10/99

50 GREAT MONOLOGS

FOR STUDENT ACTORS

A workbook of comedy characterizations for students

BILL MAJESKI

MERIWETHER PUBLISHING LTD.
Colorado Springs, Colorado

Meriwether Publishing Ltd., Publisher
P.O. Box 7710
Colorado Springs, CO 80933

Editor: Arthur Zapel
Typesetting: Sharon Garlock
Cover design: Michelle Zapel Gallardo

Library of Congress Cataloging-in-Publication Data

Majeski, Bill.
50 great monologs for student actors.

    Rev. ed. of: 25 great monologs for student actors. 1985.
    1.Humorous recitations. 2. American wit and humor. 3. Monologues. I. Majeski, Bill. 25 great monologs for student actors. II. Title. III. Title: Fifty great monologs for student actors.
PN4251.M34   1987   812'.54   87-14103
ISBN 0-916260-43-7 (pbk.)

7   8   9   03   02   01   00   99

TABLE OF CONTENTS

NOTE: The numerals running vertically down the left margin of each page of dialog are for the convenience of the director. With these, he/she may easily direct attention to a specific passage.

#1

History of New York City

CAST: Monologist — male or female

PROP: A list with items to be read as an aid for the performer, if desired.

MONOLOGIST: Nothing like expanding your horizons of knowledge, I always say — which is why I don't get invited to too many parties.

However, today, I carry on with my teaching. I'm going to bring to you a capsule history of New York City.

(Reads now from list.) **1614 — Captain Adrian Block drew the first map of the then so-called New Netherlands. On the map, Greenwich Village was upside-down, backwards and rather strange. It remains that way today.**

1626 — Peter Minuit, director-general of the island, purchases Manhattan for twenty-four dollars. Today, it is easily worth three times that amount.

1640 — War with Indians breaks out. First toupee store opens.

1642 — City Tavern is established. This later becomes City Hall. Many office-holders never realize it's been changed.

1653 — First municipal government provides for a leader known as a schout, along with two burgomasters and five schepens. This beats everything except a royal flush.

1657 — Great-burgher rights and small-burgher rights are established. Great burghers are acquired with a payment of fifty guilders; small burghers are twenty-five guilders. With French fries — twenty-five cents extra.

1671 — Somebody steals Peter Stuyvesant's wooden leg and makes him hopping mad.

1684 — First session of Court of General Sessions of New York is held. Five judges are convicted.

1690 — First post office is established in Manhattan, manned by three employees. Today it takes twelve men to do the job.

1699 — New York City population is four thousand four hundred and thirty-six. None of these are alive today, due to a pestilence.

1798 — Major General John Andres is captured with plans of West Point in his pocket. He claims they are signals for the big Army-Navy game.

1807 — Robert Fulton demonstrates his first steamboat. Unfortunately, he demonstrated it at Twenty-third Street and Fifth Avenue.

1815 — Health Board urges people be vaccinated to protect against smallpox — dart games flourish.

1883 — Brooklyn Bridge opens. Manhattanites ask why.

1888 — Great Blizzard drops twenty-one inches of snow on New York. If things go well, the Sanitation Department hopes to have it all removed by next Thursday.

1918 — Spanish influenza epidemic breaks out. Daughters of American Revolution protests against foreign elements in country.

1931 — Tallest building in the world, the Empire State Building, is completed. Brooklynites ask why.

1939 — First Good Humor man is beaten up and pummeled with Popsicle™ sticks.

1949 — Mayor opens up first home for unwed muggers.

1964 — New York becomes the first city where you can hear cries for help in seven different languages.

1   1972 — In an effort to combat crime, "Shorty"
2 Blim, circus midget, takes job riding shotgun on a
3 supermarket cart.
4   1973 to present — Nothing has happened in New
5 York of any importance.
6   Thank you.
7 *(MONOLOGIST exits.)*
8
9
10
11
12
13
14
15
16
17
18
19
20
21
22
23
24
25
26
27
28
29
30
31
32
33
34
35

How I Spent My Summer Vacation

CAST: Monologist — male or female

PROPS: A small notebook from which Monologist can read when describing dogs.

MONOLOGIST: Miss *(Or Mr.)* _____
(Name of teacher) **asked us to describe what we did during our summer vacation. So here goes.**

I spent most of the summer with my grandparents, who live way out in the country, two hundred miles from here. Oh, we had plenty of easy-going fun and activities in the afternoon and evenings, but the most exciting times happened during the mornings.

Early every morning, I would take a brisk walk or jog along nearly deserted country roads. I wanted a bit of exercise in the cool, crisp air before the cars began spraying the air with noxious fumes. But nearly every morning, I encountered trouble — a strange dog.

Do you realize that the average cocker spaniel immediately doubles in size and grows six extra teeth when you confront it alone on a country back road?

Not only cocker spaniels — *all* **dogs. From out of nowhere, you're threatened by a lunging, barking, four-footed creature you thought existed only in picture books of dinosaurs.**

Your fear shows immediately . . . the sweating palms, the tingling feeling at the back of the neck.

Now he's leaping, lunging, crouching, circling, growling. He means business — and his business is . . . *you!*

Now I don't mean those cuddly little poodles. I'm talking about dogs. Real big dogs. Monsters, in fact.

After six weeks of those confrontations in the country, I've compiled a catalog of creatures I've met that might cross *your* path when you're out for a casual stroll some bright morning. You'll probably recognize some of these right away. *(Takes out paper or notebook and can read the description of the dogs from it.)*

Alsatian Meat Hound — This dog grows shoulder-high to everyone. He was originally bred to fight fire trucks and Sherman tanks, but is willing to attack a human if the mood strikes. Won't bother you if he's well-fed — about half a horse a day.

Wire-Haired Wolf Dog — He has a wire-haired temper to match. He will only bite people during months that have the letter "R" in them. Or months that don't. Given to whimsical eccentricities — like running amok. Best defense: a plane ticket to Montreal.

North American Big-Mouth Barker — His bark is worse than his bite — unless he bites. He is readily identifiable, because he comes in black, brown, gray and blood-red.

Standard Water Buffalo Hound — This dog chases water buffaloes — and, more important, catches them. Exceedingly carnivorous, which means he is capable of eating cars. Best defense: Climb a tree and shout as loud as you can for *(Shouts.)* **Hellllpppp!** *(Go through motions as described.)*

Now what do you do when approached by a leering canine on a lonely road? Try to fake him out of position and run for it? No. Never. He's too fast.

Smile cheerily? No good. He may mistake it for a smirk, and then where are you?

Try rolling over and playing dead? No-no. If things go wrong, you won't have to do any playing.

1   Pet experts say the best maneuver is to stop for
2   a while. Look away. *(NARRATOR continues through these*
3   *motions as he/she says them.)*
4   Staring at the dog *(Stares hard)* may be considered
5   a slap-in-the-face challenge. Then walk slowly away *(Does*
6   *so)*, hoping the dog will realize you aren't invading his
7   turf and will do the same. *(Returns to position.)* But turning
8   your back on a big barking dog takes willpower that few
9   people possess. I know I don't have it.
10   I enjoyed my vacation and want to go back. But
11   this time I'll be better prepared. I told my Uncle Charley
12   about my problem. He suggested when I walk I take along
13   with me a very large animal as a walking companion.
14   Now I think that's a super idea. *(Pauses.)* Anybody know
15   where I can buy a good used rhinocerous?
16
17
18
19
20
21
22
23
24
25
26
27
28
29
30
31
32
33
34
35

#3

A Big-City Newspaper Story

CAST: Monologist — male

PROPS: Desk. Clothing box on desk. Pair of pants inside box. Telephone. (General notes: The speaker or monologist is Brant Kellmer. He is the editor. He will move around as he speaks, introducing imagined staff members.)

MONOLOGIST: You are now looking at the city room of the *Metropolitan Splendid World,* a big-city newspaper, the heartbeat of the city, the lifeblood of humanity, the ... well, you get the idea.

I'm Brant Kellmer, editor of this great newspaper, and it is a great newspaper and we have great people.

Our building is situated in the famous Nursery Rhyme Building, directly across from the state capitol and the fabled Mother Goose Farm. People come from miles around to inspect our plant and tour the building to see how a dynamic newspaper operates in the name of freedom of the press. Now let me introduce you to a few of our staff members. *(He moves as he introduces people.)* This is one of our new additions, Brenda Berdoo. When Brenda first came to the *Splendid World,* she was so inexperienced, she thought a deadline was when the telephone went out of order. Her byline is read by thousands of people. Some of them even read the stories under it. *(He walks over to another part of the stage.)*

This is Ed Squinch, our city editor. Hard-boiled, tough, cynical, wordly, wise-cracking, cantankerous — which is why lots of people don't particularly like him.

Ed has ink in his blood, which is fine unless you

1	happen to need a transfusion. *(MONOLOGIST moves to*
2	*another area.)* **This is Leona Belt, our rewrite chief.**
3	**Recently, she did a feature on the 1950 World Series,**
4	**rewriting it completely, giving a different ending.**
5	*(Goes to another area.)* **And this is kindly old Fred**
6	**Kindly, lovable copy desk chief. He once wrote a 10,000**
7	**word article all about the second floor of this building.**
8	**He was going to write about the third floor, but that's**
9	**another story.**
10	*(To another area.)* **And this is our sob-sister, Marcia**
11	**Foolscap, a fine newspaper gal. Last year, she went to**
12	**jail for three weeks because she wouldn't reveal the**
13	**source of her story. Then she went back voluntarily**
14	**because she fell in love with the warden.**
15	**Besides our great people, another reason for our**
16	**greatness is that some of our stories are actually based**
17	**on fact.** *(Sound: phone rings. MONOLOGIST speaks as he*
18	*heads for it.)* **A typical new day is just beginning in a great**
19	**newspaper which upholds the freedom of the press.** *(Into*
20	*phone. Listens. Repeats.)* **I see. Fire. Jack be nimble, Jack**
21	**be quick and . . . didn't quite make it. Kicked the**
22	**candlestick over and the fire is out of control. Where?**
23	**OK.** *(Hangs up phone. Calls to imaginary work area.)* **Send**
24	**Tompkins to 321 Taper Street, fire. Take a photographer.**
25	*(Phone rings. MONOLOGIST picks it up and speaks into phone.)*
26	**Yeah.** *(Listens, repeats.)* **Tom, Tom the piper's son, stole a**
27	**pig and away he run. Call back when you get more.** *(Hangs*
28	*up phone. Speaks to area.)* **We've got a pig-snatcher running**
29	**loose. Probably somebody who wants to throw a luau.**
30	*(Phone rings. MONOLOGIST speaks into phone.)* **Yeah.**
31	*(Listens.)* **Sure, we're interested in water conservation.**
32	*(Repeats.)* **Big story? Go. Story about what? Three men in**
33	**a tub? Sorry, pal, we don't do weirdo stories.** *(Hangs up*
34	*phone and shakes his head. To audience.)* **In this game, you**
35	**have to make instant decisions — even if it takes all day.**

1	*(Phone rings. MONOLOGIST answers.)* **OK, gotcha.** *(Hangs*
2	*up phone, calls out to staffer.)* **Cancellation. Water polo finals**
3	**have been called off at Mother Goose Stadium. One of the**
4	**horses drowned.** *(Starts over to package on the desk. He is*
5	*about to open it when the phone rings. To audience.)* **Have to**
6	**go to the governor's ball. Hope the tailor did a good job**
7	**pressing my pants.** *(Into phone.)* **Yeah? Great.** *(Hangs up.*
8	*Calls to space.)* **They caught Tom with the pig. Give me**
9	**about six graphs.** *(Starts over to package on desk, but the phone*
10	*rings again. Into phone.)* **Yes, I'm Brant Kellmer. Ah, you're**
11	**the piper. Yes. Tom Tom is your son. Well, they caught**
12	**him with the pig he stole. Right.** *(Listens.)* **Of course we**
13	**can't do that. We can't kill the story. I don't care how**
14	**important you are. We print all the news. It's called**
15	**freedom of the press.** *(Hangs up phone.)* **The nerve of that**
16	**guy.** *(Finally gets to box, opens it. Takes out pair of pants and*
17	*inspects them.)* **Great job. Wonder if he's going to soak me.**
18	*(Picks up phone, dials. Speaks into phone.)* **Rumpelstiltskin's**
19	**Tailor Shop. Hi, Rumpel. Say, you did a great job. How**
20	**much do I owe you?** *(Listens.)* **Really, that's very nice of**
21	**you. No charge. Free. You're my man, Rumpel.** *(Hangs up.*
22	*To audience. Puts pants over his arm.)* **Didn't charge a cent.**
23	**And that, folks, is another stirring example of freedom**
24	**of the press.** *(He exits, inspecting the pants as he does so.)*
25	
26	
27	
28	
29	
30	
31	
32	
33	
34	
35	

#4

The Fanatical Spectator

CAST: Narrator — On stage or off; male or female; Monologist — male. Can take any voice he prefers, though a typical know-it-all fan voice is preferred.

PROPS: Chair or bench, bag of popcorn.

NARRATOR: No doubt about it, ballplayers are taking great abuse these days. They are yelled at, cursed at and have heavy objects thrown at them by fanatical spectators in the stands.

This is very tough to take when you have a hard baseball whizzing in your direction at 90 miles per hour.

Imagine if a bunch of loud-mouthed hostile viewers vented their wrath at a plumber while he was working, or a bookkeeper or even a surgeon.

Picture this. The setting: A hospital surgical arena with a packed gallery. "The Star Spangled Banner" is played. Doctor Harry Thompson is at the table with three scalpels, taking some practice swings. The patient, wrapped in sheets, lies, under medication, on the table. The operation begins. A pushy fan with popcorn arrives late and bulls his way into a seat.

MONOLOGIST: Appendectomy, eh? Who's working? Let's see. *(Squints.)* Number twenty-seven. Thompson? What's he doing here? He's an eye-ear-nose-and-whatchacallit man. What's he doing in a belly? *(Shouts.)* Thompson, ya bum, ya! *(To guy next to him.)* Hey, buddy, look at that Humpty-Dumpty, will ya? Look how he's got those clamps! *(Shouts.)* Ya bum, ya! *(To next guy.)* Where's Swenson? You know, that big blond doc? He should be here. *(Pauses, listening.)* **What do you mean, he can't win the big ones? He was twelve and three last yea..**

Look at that klutz. Right in his hands and he dropped it! That Thompson thinks an operation is a success if he can find all his instruments later.

(Shouts.) **Not that way! The other side, the other side!** *(To other fan.)* **Get him outta there.** *(Shouts.)* **We want Swenson! We want Swenson!** *(To other fan.)* **Stamp your feet and start yelling, Mac. We need Swenson.** *(MONOLOGIST starts rhythmic feet stamping.)*

(Claps hands happily.) **Ah . . . here he is. Now we go.** *(Shouts.)* **Hey, Swenson, baby, show him where it's at.**

(To next fan.) **Huh? How about that? Did I tell you? Look at that style.** *(Shouts.)* **How to work, baby! Way to go.** *(To next fan.)* **Can that man cut?** *(Shouts.)* **Go, Swen, baby. Deep . . . .deeper . . . move it, now, Swen! We're rolling now. Beauty! Go inside, now . . . cut . . . cut . . . cut . . .** *(Silence — long pause.)*

They waited too long to bring Swenson in . . . I mean he's a starter, not a reliever . . . Well . . . you can't win 'em all . . . *(MONOLOGIST gets up and exits.)*

#5

Harley Henderson's Airlines
for the Oldsters

CAST: Monologist — male; Narrator — male or female.

NARRATOR: *(Offstage.)* **Student flying fares are a bargain, and they keep getting lower and lower. Great. But what about the elderly? They need a break, too. And now it's here. Yes, through the good graces of Harley Henderson Airlines, oldsters can fly at reduced rates. Here now is a spokesman for HH Airlines.**

MONOLOGIST: Hi, oldsters. I want to tell you about the Harley Henderson Airlines' policy for you.

Planning on taking a trip soon? Tired of smoothing wrinkles or whittling crutches and want to get away from it all? Fly Harley.

Just listen. If you're over seventy and can prove it by a birth certificate or wounds suffered at San Juan Hill, Harley offers one-half off regular fare — two-thirds off if you sit with your legs crossed so you take up less plane room.

Harley offers such money-saving bargains because he has an unscheduled airline. Actually, the take-offs are scheduled — the landings are unscheduled. But that's where the fun is, right? Sure.

Harley doesn't waste good money on extravagant foods. When you dine with Harley, you get a mouth-watering bowl of gruel, a macaroon and a potato-salad sculpture of a train wreck.

Why should Harley spend money hiring beautiful stewardesses when he can pick Hoboken waterfront rejects for a song? When Harley's girls ask, "Coffee, tea or me?", they keep running out of coffee and tea. Another saving for passengers.

Harley thinks of everything to conserve and pass the savings on to you. When his overweight stewardesses aren't flying, he rents their dresses out as windsocks and that adds to his overall income. You profit.

Talk about unique entertainment. None of those stale first-run movies when you fly Harley. No *sirree*. Harley has a hostess come around every two minutes with a viewing machine showing old "Smiling Jack" and "Tailspin Tommy" comic strips. Another saving.

Harley is a traditionalist when it comes to safety. None of those new-fangled radar units or altimeters. But to make sure the plane is landing into the wind, old Harley straps an aging stewardess onto the wing to check out the wind direction.

Harley likes to boast — "We haven't lost a plane yet. A stewardess or two, yes, but not one plane."

None of those sleek, expensive jet planes for Harley. No, sir. But his planes are airworthy, from their balsam wood pontoons, right up to the propellor on the pilot's beanie.

Some of the pilots are student drivers, as the required sign says. Now they've passed all the flying tests; failing only the written tests. But after all, how important is a written exam when you're in a spin heading for a mountaintop at three hundred miles per hour?

And another thing, oldsters — friendliness abounds on Harley's flights. On rainy nights, all thirteen passengers huddle together in a corner to keep from getting drenched by the rain coming in through that gaping hole in the center of the roof. Oh, the joy, the singing, the happiness and the togetherness make you feel as if you're right back home at a family picnic.

Have someone drop a note for you to get full

1   information for our rates.
2   **Remember, fly Harley. See you at the airport.** *(He*
3   *exits.)*
4
5
6
7
8
9
10
11
12
13
14
15
16
17
18
19
20
21
22
23
24
25
26
27
28
29
30
31
32
33
34
35

#6

Personality Components, Ready to Wear

CAST: Monologist, preferably male. Narrator — Offstage.

PROPS: None. (Possibly a desk and chair if it aids the performer.)

NARRATOR: People today are picking up new and used internal organs at the drop of a heart. You know it's only a matter of time before they'll be able to go to their friendly neighborhood skull technician and outfit themselves with the very latest personality components.

Watch now as this young man enters the office of Doctor Farley Tiffner. Meet Edgar Wheary.
(MONOLOGIST enters, goes to desk if one is to be used.)

MONOLOGIST: Hello, doctor. I'd like to pick up a complex. I wonder if you've got something that would suit me.
(MONOLOGIST will do a lot of listening and repeating doctor's remarks.) **I think I'd like something to match the blue funk I often find myself in.**

(Listens.) **Hmmm ...** *(Repeats.)* **A special in guilt complexes this month, with emphasis on focal points of turmoil and various disturbances.**

You see, I don't want anything big or showy. *(Listens, repeats.)* **You have one in stock that disturbs me tremendously because I'm not making as much money as the man across the street.** *(Nods knowledgeably.)* **Yes, I know envy is big this year.** *(Listens, repeats.)* **Hmmm. Comes with flare-ups on the spasmodic basis and dual emotional outlets.** *(Listens.)* **But, doctor, it seems everyone has that these days. I'd like something a bit out of the ordinary.** *(Repeats, nods.)* **Your repression numbers are**

moving fast. This one allows me to grouse a bit and it creates the impression that I'm sublimating my delicate artistic tendencies to compete in the workaday world. Sounds good.

What else? I can make thinking sounds, utter pseudo-philosophical statements about the world situation, political climate, the fast tempo of living and the decline of good hot cross buns.

That sounds good, but will it hurt? *(Listens, repeats.)* Only when I preen. Frankly, I like to preen. *(Repeats.)* Something cheaper? OK, lay it on me. *(Listens, repeats.)* One you'll let go for a song. Matches, easy to use, and I won't have any side effects. Popular with all. It's called the Acro. I'll be afraid of toppling off Wilt Chamberlain. You're using your special Acro now and you won't get within ten feet of the window.

You see, I don't like heights anyway. It would just be a waste of money.

(Listens, repeats.) You have a new model in today? You got it from a young poet in Greenwich Village who gave it all up and went into his father's carbuncle and cyanide business? It does what? Elicits sympathy from older women. You feel it's just the thing for a swinging bachelor? Doesn't sound bad.

Anything more personal? *(Listens, repeats.)* The Bystander model component. It will give me an inordinate fear of being left out of conversations. So I'll talk more and become aggressive, snarl a lot and I'll get myself heard and respected. I'll be a *tiger*.

Tiger. That's me. Don't bother to wrap it up. I'll wear it home. So long, boy. *(MONOLOGIST strides out very aggressively, growling fiercely as he does so.)*

#7

"Peyton Place" Revisited

CAST: Monologist — preferably male.

PROPS: None. (Though an old *TV Guide* might be helpful.)

MONOLOGIST: This dissertation is aimed specifically at you older folks out there — teen-agers.

Some of you might recall the glory years of television's situation comedies. Shows like the "Dick Van Dyke Show," "The Honeymooners," "The Andy Griffith Show" — all fine comedies. The most talked-about program though, was not a comedy — at least not intentionally — it was called "Peyton Place."

But it ended rather suddenly, and viewers wondered what happened to all those wonderful, warped weirdos who populated the screen on "Peyton Place."

People who liked the show were left steaming because they didn't know what happened to the mainstays of their program, which was based on a novel set in New Hampsire. New Hampsire?! Yes, New Hampshire.

As a public service, I'm going to try to tell you just what became of those lovely people in Peyton Place, New Hampshire.

Here are some of the questions viewers asked most: *(MONOLOGIST may read from TV listings if so desired.)*

"Whatever became of Allison?" You remember pretty Allison. I am happy to say that Allison is alive and well and working as a guidance counselor for Eddie Murphy.

"Who would get all the Peyton money?" The

money would go to an association known as the Amalgamated Truss Fund for Tired Weight Lifters.

"What about Lew Miles' arrest on a hit-and-run charge in New York?" You younger people probably won't recall Lew Miles, but he was there. About the hit-and-run business — fortunately, the man he hit died, and in New York, murder is a lesser charge than hit-and-run. Lew was given a ten-day suspended sentence and forced to watch reruns of "Gilligan's Island."

"When last heard of, Rodney was paralyzed. Did he recover?" I'm happy to say Rodney recovered completely. He is living quietly as a bunny tender in Hugh Hefner's House of Worship.

"At last report, Rita was about to give birth. Boy or girl? Twins?" Rita gave birth to a utility infielder and a small motorcycle.

"Did Ann Howard jump or fall to her death from the cliff? If she was pushed, who pushed her?" Ann Howard fell from the cliff. However, she wasn't killed. She pulled the ripcord in time and her pajamas opened up, causing her to flutter safely into Tom Selleck's apartment. She has not been seen again.

"Did Susan and Tom ever reconcile and settle down in New Hampshire?" Yes. Susan reconciled with Ann, and Tom reconciled with Rodney. Wild. And all in New Hampshire.

(Looks at watch.) Excuse me. If I rush out now, I'll have time to catch the next train to New Hampshire. *(Exits.)*

#8

Trains of Nightmarish Thoughts

CAST: Male Monologist is preferable for this one, though a female would probably do just as well. The performer might want to work from a train schedule as a prop and possible script aid.

MONOLOGIST: Do trains bother you? More specifically, train schedules. They get to me. Let me tell you about a recent experience I had.

It was weird. Scary. Eerie. Perhaps it was the weather. Perhaps it was the whirl and swirl of today's up-tempo times. Perhaps my body shirt was meant for some other body. I don't know. I only know that it happened. It may have been a bad dream.

I had to go to Port Washington on Long Island. There is a Port Washington. I knew that much. I went down to the railroad station. At 9:15 a.m., a train pulled into the station, wrecking it. I went to another station and groped for a schedule, which seemed to be on a floating rack. The sign above said I was in Syosset.

The schedule had all the information I needed. A train left Syosset at 10 a.m. and arrived in Port Washington at 11 a.m. Simple? Easy? No. A footnote caught me. Footnote A — "Does not run today." OK, you figure it out.

Next train out of Syosset was 10:30. The schedule said it arrived back in Syosset at 11:30. Didn't say where it was going. I was getting nowhere.

Next train — noon. Another footnote. Footnote T — "Traitor's Special — runs only on Benedict Arnold's birthday."

Next train — 1:30 p.m. Footnote D. "D hit into a

double play for pitcher in eighth inning." The 2:45 carried Footnote C. "Miss one turn, go back ten spaces. Do not pass Go. Five o'clock train. Footnote M. "M is for the million things you gave me."

I stopped singing after two choruses and found a train leaving for Port Washington at 6:30, due to arrive at 7:30. I boarded the train. A man with a basket sold me a cardboard sandwich and a carton of chalk water for three dollars and eighty cents. It was painful and expensive.

I sat back and waited and waited for the train to leave.

Then the conductor came to my seat, smiling broadly. That's trouble. It's bad news when a conductor smiles.

"Sorry, Mac," he said, "Tough luck. The train broke down and can't run . . . but the *station* just left for Port Washington."

It *was* a bad dream. It turned into a nightmare of hellish design. Then I saw a sign overhead. It said this railroad was taken over by the Long Island Railroad. And now the *real* fears set in. What if it all *wasn't* a bad dream?

Something to think about late at night.

Thank you.

By the way, the next train for Port Washington won't be going there. So drop into my place — we'll all have some fun. Take care. *(Exits.)*

#9

Letter to an Escaper

CAST: Monologist — well-dressed male. He is a prison warden dictating a letter to his secretary.

MONOLOGIST: A while back, a British prisoner of "fantastic strength" escaped from Dartmoor Prison. He is Frank Mitchell, a giant of a man known to his intimates and crime buffs as Britain's Mad Axman.

Well, sir, being locked up and all that, Frank got irritated and broke out.

Now Britain's home secretary, Roy Jenkins, sensing that a sulking, hulking giant might do tremendous damage to the public-at-large, wrote a letter to the newspapers offering Mitchell his release from prison, legally, if he returned peacefully.

Let's face it, writing a letter to a mad axman anytime is a difficult problem. How did Mr. Jenkins handle it? I can see him now.

(Dictating letter to unseen secretary.) **Dear Mad Axman. No, Dear Maniac . . . is *maniac* a synonym for *axman* in this case, Miss Dudley? Dear Mr. Mitchell . . . no, too chummy. Suppose we go with "To Whom It May Concern" and be done with it.**

As per your recent breakout from Dartmoor Prison due to real or fancied difficulties, I would like you to please consider the following offer: lay down your ax and come back to Dartmoor.

Once you show your good faith by coming back inside the prison bars you bent so handily, we can work out something giving you your official release and send you on your merry way. Possibly even a long vacation to

Jamaica or some other distant spot can be worked out. Sound all right, Frank?

Dartmoor really isn't a bad prison. Anytime you take three thousand murderers, embezzlers, con men, rowdies and yes, even, mad axmen — no offense — you're bound to have some bad apples.

Your room is the same way you left it — in a shambles. The bed is torn in half, the walls are kicked in and the lighting fixtures have been eaten away. But if a man can't work off some steam in prison, then, by heaven, where can he do so?

Remember the fun in shop? Remember the nice ashtray you made out of Stretch Morrison's head? Of course, Stretch isn't really Stretch anymore. Thanks to your constant artful pounding, he's been hammered down considerably and he makes a nice conversation piece when the wardens get together and flick their cigar ashes into his skull. We talk about it all the time.

And how about the fine food? Remember the great performance you put on in the mess hall last spring, eating ten entire meals, nineteen paper napkins and part of Ed McMartin's right elbow? Well, let me tell you that *Lefty* McMartin bears no grudge. But a word of caution — old Lefty has been made chief cook.

However, there is nothing to worry about. You can eat your meals with the wardens — or any place you want to, for that matter. We're not batting on a sticky wicket, old boy.

So think it over, Axman. Let bygones be bygones and come home. Hoping we can bury the hatchet.

Sincerely,

(Signed)

Home Secretary Roy Jenkins

(MONOLOGIST takes bow and exits.)

#10

The Last Few Days of Shopping
Before Christmas

CAST: Monologist — either male or female.

(MONOLOGIST enters.)

MONOLOGIST: Employees ... attention please. I am
Lancelot Boggins, your general manager.

In ten minutes, the door will open and the mob
of last-minute shoppers will come streaming in. Some of
you will be injured. Some will never be seen again.

It's also possible some of you may be battered
beyond recognition ... which is the reason for those
numbered tags on your toes.

If you feel you're not up to this battle, get out
now! But once your name is on the chicken list, you'll
never work for a big store again. Those who stay — be
ready!

Your crash helmets and bullet-proof vests are
over at the armament table.

Check your first aid book. Pay particular
attention to the chapter entitled "How to Give Mouth-to-
Mouth Resuscitation without Getting Emotionally
Involved."

A special reminder to Mr. Benson. No mistletoe
hanging over the doorway to the ladies' dress
department. Remember the stink those blue noses from
the vice squad made last year? Remember, there's no way
you can identify a policewoman once she slips out of her
uniform.

A warning to all hands — don't let mothers
deposit their kids in Lost and Found. They forget them.

1	On purpose! Last year we got stuck with forty-seven of
2	those rotten ... er ... *cute* little tykes. Fortunately we
3	managed to place most of them with nice families, but
4	we still have a half-dozen kids *nobody* wants.
5	Remember, customers steal! Girls handling
6	hairpieces — wigs are easy to lift. Don't accuse anyone.
7	We can get sued. Simply use your electric fans as an aid
8	to detection.
9	Now, finally, all toy department personnel — don't
10	let grown men play with Barbie dolls. They have a
11	tendency to develop a terrific crush on Barbie. Last year
12	we had to toss out a grown man kicking and screaming.
13	Do you think it's easy taking a Barbie doll away from Mr.
14	T?
15	Thank you, and *go get 'em*!
16	
17	
18	
19	
20	
21	
22	
23	
24	
25	
26	
27	
28	
29	
30	
31	
32	
33	
34	
35	

#11

Musical Intros

CAST: Monologist — either male or female. Probably would be better if the intros are done in a very clipped, almost stilted manner.

Production Note: This requires either a piano or some other instrument, or a phonograph handled Offstage. The music following the introductions can, and should be, brief, perhaps eight bars at the most.

MONOLOGIST: **This opus you are about to hear was written by the notorious Richard Vistaker in exactly ninety days — the time he was sentenced to prison for breach of assault. He had promised to beat up on a masochist and then broke his word, a misdemeanor in Memphis. However, it happened in Annapolis, Maryland, where it is a felony. Vistaker's fierce, yet subdued, musical style is clearly in evidence here, particularly in the second chorus, where the reeds stop playing and start again. Something sophisticated music lovers will appreciate.**

Though confined to his cell, Vistaker's love of the outdoors is shown in the third chorus by the chattering woodwinds and a strangely muted brass, an effect created by the use of a large bird stuffed in the bell of a trombone ... and a small bird stuffed in the mouth of the trombonist. Listen now ... to "Jubilee Fishmarket." *(Musical Interlude.)*

"Honeymoon Suite, Hey, Baby," by Jimmy Teardown was written several years ago for the organ. However, the organ didn't want it, so it was turned over to the bass drum, along with some breakfast cereal and a box of chocolates.

Teardown, who had been married seven times in twenty-six years, with two years off for good behavior, composed this sprightly number after witnessing a tall lady combing her hair during a monsoon.

The haunting tones of the oboe weave a sinuous melody as we hear an interpolation of "There's a Small Hotel" played by flautists against a background of traffic noises.

Here then, is "Honeymoon Suite, Hey, Baby." *(Brief musical interlude.)*

"Long Live the Prince of Urbanization," a startling jazz symphony, was written specifically for an outdoor summer concert in New York's Central Park.

The searing, soaring tones of the reeds are meant to simulate the screams of mugging victims which often rend the night air.

The woodblock solo which leads off the second movement represents the clip-clopping of the mounted policeman who has heard there is big trouble at the west end of the park and is galloping madly toward the *east* end of the park.

One of the most memorable passages in musicdom is heard shortly after with the near-celestial blending of strings, tympani and breadsticks played on the side of a sheepskin drawn tightly over a veiled harridan.

Composer Harley Resenfree has this to say of his own work: "I don't talk to strangers."

And now, listen please to "Long Live the Prince of Urbanization." *(Brief musical interlude.)*

"Excerpts from Unrequited Boredom" by Ransom Bangaloo, is a starkly realistic opera which was presented first in France and then buried in a common grave until it was exhumed by a team of dancing gravediggers.

The mournful wails describe the lurid romance

of Pasgate Nickelbee, a poor French shrugmaster whose hobby was bathtub plugs. Conflict comes early when we learn that Pasgate has not a tooth in his head and is trying to grow some. He falls in love with Brisket Donovan, Australia's only female swineherd.

Their whirlwind romance is signified by the unique blending of bassoons, Dick Stabile's C-melody sax and a pocket comb . . . played while still in the pocket of an ice cream vendor.

Here now, the opera — "Excerpts from Unrequited Boredom." *(Brief musical interlude.)*

No program of classical music is complete without Ed Benson's glorious "Putting on the Rich."

Benson, whose background was one of poverty, detested anyone with money, large cars or expensive eyeglasses. His mother worked as a dirigible tender, while his father took in laundry women. Benson expressed his hostility through his music, as you will hear soon.

The harmonic distillation of the final sixteen bars is created by a cellist hitting high C, a clarinetist hitting a low F sharp and Benson, himself, hitting the conductor over the head with the bass fiddle during the recording session. The conductor, who was wealthy — Benson only whacked the rich — still suffers occasionally from fiddle pains especially in the damp weather.

As for Benson, he has disappeared completely. He stands five feet, six inches, weighs one hundred and fifty pounds and was last seen wearing a string tie and matching Argyle socks.

Listen closely now to the delicate, yet brutal, sounds of "Putting on the Rich." *(Brief musical interlude.)*

Hope you enjoyed the music and . . . thanks for listening.

#12

What Does Your Handwriting Tell You?

CAST: Monologist — male or female. Announcer — Offstage.

PROPS: Desk and a batch of big cards with various graffiti written
on them.

ANNOUNCER: *(Offstage, if the director feels it's necessary.)*
Graphology seems to have peaked and is now on
the decline as far as figuring our future and/or character
through handwriting. This is known as graphology. And,
along those lines, let us bring to you, at no great expense,
our expert, Mr. Farley Graphology. Why not compare
your handwriting with the examples and give yourself
an instant analysis. *(Presenting.)* **And here is Mr.
Graphology.** *(GRAPHOLOGY pick up first card from the pile
on his desk, looks at it and then presents it for audience approval.
Cards should vaguely refer to the descriptive analysis offered by
MR. GRAPHOLOGY.)*

GRAPHOLOGY: *(Holding up card.)* **Now here we have what
they call the heavy crossing of the T's, not to be confused
with the crossing of the Nile . . .which can get you in deep
water. Now, what does heavy crossing of the T's mean?**
(Whimsically.) **I asked you first. It reveals willpower,
impulsiveness and a slight tendency to stumble. You're
inclined to rush headlong into things, like business deals
and spinning propellors.**

   Now *(Holding up card for audience.)*, **here we have
what we like to call the short cross of the T. Or, as it is
sometimes called, the weak-side off-tackle play. If you
write like this, it implies you are indecisive and filled
with doubts about even life's smaller problems. Like —**

should you tip a man who guides you to the center of the George Washington Bridge and says: "It's OK to leap after 3 p.m."? If a man sneezes down your collar, should you say "Gesundheit?" Also, beware of falling off buildings on Thursdays.

(Holding up card.) Notice the light dotting of I's. They are light . . . not heavy at all. I can lift it easily. This usually connotes great powers of nothing except a weak hand. It hints at a weakness of willpower and a lack of willpower in everything except weaknesses. It indicates self-hate, inward desires of questionable taste and some clearing in the Northwest portion of the state. Also, don't overeat.

(Holds up card.) As you can see, here we have the big round dotting of the I's. You probably have weird fantasies. It is best to avoid half-drawn window shades and the corner of Fifth Avenue and 42nd Street on windy days. You have a tendency to yodel in crowded elevators, and that bodes ill luck for your future. You possibly are the type that would go to the old folks' home and wax floors before the annual dance.

(Holds up card.) This shows an upward trend in writing across the page. The person is an optimistic type, so much so in fact that many people think he's downright foolish. For instance, three people who wrote on an upward grade last year were run over by bulldozers as they stood in the street as they tried to find the pot of gold at the end of a rainbow. You see good in everything, even bubonic plague and windstorms. Face reality. Kick a uniformed attendant and don't run. Let a smile be your umbrella and you'll catch pneumonia. Straighten out, simpleton.

(Holds up card.) Ah, a down slant. This is more like it. Pessimism is your weakness. Don't think everyone in sight will haul off and whack you. Only two or three will

give you a belt. Watch out for small fires in your hair. You seem to be the type who'll drive by a lonely highway and give hitchhikers dirty looks. Remember, it's nice to give people boosts — jab 'em with a bayonet if it makes you feel better. Don't smoke in wind tunnels.

(Holds up sign which says "Stick 'em up.") This means today will be a bad day for you.

#13

The World's Smartest Man — Mr. Know-It-All

CAST: Announcer — Offstage, if desired, or a man or woman making a brief appearance and then exiting. Monologist (Mr. Know-It-All).

PROPS: Table, set with blue or white cards, from which Mr. Know-It-All can read questions.

ANNOUNCER: **And now, knowledge fans, here he is, Mr. Know-It-All.** *(KNOW-IT-ALL enters, in whatever type of outfit the director feels will heighten the comic quotient of the scene.)*

KNOW-IT-ALL: **Let me read the first card containing, logically enough, the first question.** *(Reads.)* **It's from a listener in Putney, Vermont. "How many Indians came to the first Thanksgiving dinner?" Answer — it was attended by three hundred and twenty-one Indian braves — and fourteen Indian cowards.** *(Reads from card.)* **Here's one from J.P. in Burlington, Iowa. Sort of a grammatical stickler. "Which word means neither brother nor sister?" Answer — the word which means neither brother nor sister is *giggle* — which means to laugh in a silly manner.**

(Reads from card.) **Here's one from T.T. in Tecumsah, Oklahoma. "Do all mountain ranges run north and south?" Answer — mountain ranges do *not* run. They are stationary. Ask anybody.**

(Reads from card.) **Here's a query from R.B. of Beltsville, Maryland. "Can you dive into the Great Salt Lake in Utah?" Answer — not if you are standing in Maryland.**

1	*(Reads from card.)* **This is from U.P. in Sarasota,**
2	**Florida. "How much does the temperature vary in**
3	**Alaska?" Answer — it is *vary* cold.**
4	*(Reads from card.)* **From J.P. of Evansville, Indiana:**
5	**"Why do beavers make mud pies?" Answer — what *else***
6	**can you do with all that messy goo?**
7	*(Reads from card.)* **And from W.W. of Walla Walla,**
8	**Washington. "How can a person spot a lion?" Answer — a**
9	**lion has no spots. You're thinking of a leopard.**
10	*(Reads from card.)* **Here's a query from G.T. of**
11	**Detroit, Michigan, who wants to know if the Duke of**
12	**Wellington was a hardy soldier. Answer — no — he was**
13	**an English soldier.**
14	*(Reads from card.)* **From V.M. of Lafayette,**
15	**Louisiana: "When a flying bird bumps into a building, is**
16	**the building jarred?" Answer — not half as much as the**
17	**bird.**
18	*(Reads from card.)* **A letter from U.L. of Bangor,**
19	**Maine, asks: "Where is the greatest amount of quicksand**
20	**in the world?" Answer: Diamond Shoals off Cape Hatteras**
21	**has the quickest sand in the world, covering one hundred**
22	**yards in 10.5 seconds.**
23	*(Reads from card.)* **R.M. of Meriden, Connecticut,**
24	**poses this question: "Was there ever a real person named**
25	**Cyrano de Bergerac?" Answer — yes, a jockey at Hialeah**
26	**Race Track was named Cyrano de Bergerac. His claim**
27	**to fame was that he often won by a nose.**
28	*(Reads from card.)* **From J.C. of the Bronx, New**
29	**York: "What is the largest bird in the world?" Answer —**
30	**Oscar Bird of Cincinnati is seven feet, three inches tall**
31	**and weighs four hundred and thirty-two pounds. He does**
32	**not fly.**
33	*(Reads from card.)* **From J.J. of Santa Fe, New**
34	**Mexico: "How long does a turtle live?" Answer — you call**
35	**that living?**

1   *(Reads from card.)* **And our last card from P.D. of**
2   **Scranton, Pennsylvania: "How many people work for our**
3   **federal government in Washington?" Answer — about**
4   **half of them.** *(He exits.)*
5   **ANNOUNCER:** *(Offstage.)* **Thank you very much, Know-It-All fans.**
6
7
8
9
10
11
12
13
14
15
16
17
18
19
20
21
22
23
24
25
26
27
28
29
30
31
32
33
34
35

#14

Dr. Fluegel's Medical Program

CAST: Narrator — male.

PROPS: Table with phone on it; small cards from which Narrator
will read the questions.

NARRATOR: Good day, medical fans. Well, I'm back again
to answer your questions. Before we begin, I want to say
there is no truth to the rumor that I tried to commit
suicide by throwing myself off my golf bag. I'm in perfect
health and I have a lot to live for.

All right, let's take the first question. *(With each
question, he takes a card and reads from it before answering.
Reading the questions serves as an aid for the performer in
memorizing his lines.)*

Dear Doctor Fluegal: Can athlete's foot cause a
pain in the chest? *(Answer)* Sure, if the athlete kicks you
hard enough.

Dear Doctor Fluegel: Can a man of forty develop
psychoseima cirrhosis? *(Answer)* Yes, if he's willing to
work at it.

Dear Doctor Fluegel: I've lost forty pounds in
three weeks. What's the matter with me? *(Answer)* You're
too skinny, you silly fellow. Get some meat on those
bones. You can't go walking around with a see-through
body.

Dear Doctor Fluegel: Would you please tell me
what acute infectious hepatitis is? *(Answer)* No. What's
done is done.

Dear Doctor Fluegel: Can you read my writing?
(Answer) Of course I can read your writing. Let me read

the rest of your card.

(Reading from card.) **In regard to contracting diseases as opposed to incurring a direct infection, can a chronic sickness impart an allergy and offer diagnostic symptoms which in no way can be predetermined as an integral part of the ailment? Signed G.L.** *(Answer)* **Sorry, G.L., I can't read your handwriting.**

Dear Doctor Fluegel: Do you consider soda suitable for a boy of three to drink freely? Mrs. J. *(Answer)* **No, not freely. He should pay for it like everybody else.**

Dear Doctor Fluegel: What causes one person to have curly hair and another straight? *(Answer)* **Another straight what?** *(Shakes head in dismay.)* **What's wrong with these jokers out there?**

Dear Doctor Fluegel: My father just turned eighty-six and found he no longer has the strength to use his bow and arrow set. Is this hardening of the arteries? T.C. *(Answer)* **No, it's hardening of the *archeries*. I can get silly, too, you know.**

Dear Doctor Fluegel: The other day, my brother was bitten by a rattlesnake. Shortly thereafter, he died. K.R. *(Answer)* **Sorry. Time alone will make you forget the loss of your brother.**

(Picks card.) **Ah, another one from K.R.** *(Reads.)* **Not my brother, softskull. The snake — I loved him!** *(Answer)* **Sorry, only one problem at a time.**

Dear Doctor Fluegel: I have a pilonidal cyst of the sacrococcygeal junction. Is this abnormality significant? T.L. *(Answers after doing take.)* **This gentleman uses big words. For the benefit of you other people, I won't answer the question.** *(To audience directly.)* **Smarten up, T.L., or you ain't ever gonna learn anything.**

Dear Doctor Fluegel: Is sleeping on the left side bad for the heart? *(Answer)* **Sleeping on the left side of who?** *(Questioning)* **Where do they all come from?**

1   **Dear Doctor Fluegel: What causes a sharp pain**
2 **from the throat right to the stomach?** *(Answers)* **A long**
3 **saber.**
4   **Dear Doctor Fluegel: I'm a twenty-six-year-old**
5 **blonde, very lonely but very shapely. Can you help me?**
6 *(Elated. Picks up phone, talks into it.)* **Miss Krausmeyer, hold**
7 **all calls.** *(Hangs up phone. Puts on hat, takes satchel or briefcase.*
8 *heads out smiling. To audience)* **I'm a great believer in**
9 **socialized medicine.** *(He exits.)*
10
11
12
13
14
15
16
17
18
19
20
21
22
23
24
25
26
27
28
29
30
31
32
33
34
35

#15

The Violin

CAST: Monologist — male.

MONOLOGIST: *(He comes out carrying a violin in a case. Suddenly, he points the narrow end at the audience and says:)* **Rat-tat-tat-tat-tat** ... *(Machine-gun style. He smiles sheepishly.)* **Sorry. I got carried away. You know, in the 1920s, they called the machine gun a Chicago typewriter.** *(He opens case and removes violin. Holds it out for audience to see.)* **But this is only a harmless violin. Harmless, that is, until it is played badly. Then ... murder!** *(Shakes head.)*

    Oh, permit me to introduce myself. I'm Clifford G. Clef, professor of music and green vegetables at Abnormal U. The violin is a musical instrument with four strings — G, D, E and A. Or, as they are known in musical circles — Moe, Larry, Curley and Shemp. A violin is smaller than a guitar, which has six strings. However, it is larger than a harmonica, which just about evens things up. A harp has thirty strings, but it is not considered a musical instrument.

    A violin is very safe. Last year, only four people were killed playing the violin. Investigation showed that three of the four were tone deaf.

    The violin is placed under the chin *(Demonstrates)* **just as you would place a napkin. But just try to play a tune on a napkin and see how far you'd get. On the other hand, try to wipe your mouth with a violin.**

    Charles "Zippy" Harris claimed to have invented the violin. Later, as more people began playing the instrument, Harris denied it. He later changed his name to Dizzy Dean. The violin was first introduced to the

world by Amos T. Fret. It created no excitement at all, what with Atilla the Hun and all. Without a doubt, the most famous and talented violinist was Venuti J. Pizzicato. He played concerts all over the world, but later gave up the instrument for Stradivarius reasons.

But in America, the violin gained fame rapidly, chiefly because it has a sweet tone and could be swung handily in street brawls. *(Takes a vicious swing with the violin.)* A violin has a lovely neck *(Slides hand over it)*, graceful base *(Repeats)*, high cheekbones and answers to the name Nancy.

Many stories tie the violin in with history, but the canard about Nero and his fiddle is utterly false. He did not play a violin when Rome burned — it was a bass fiddle, and he suffered severe internal injuries picking it up and putting it under his chin. His record of "Hot Time in the Old Town Tonight" is still available on the Coliseum label, with a vocal background by the Swinging Slaves.

Thank you. Goodbye . . . and keep fiddling around. *(He exits, taking violin.)*

#16

The Population Problem

CAST: Monologist — male or female. Should be dressed in something to enhance the type of tone to be used during the talk.

PROPS: None.

MONOLOGIST: Ladies and gentlemen, I've been asked to discuss with you our population problem — and if you've seen some of the weirdos I've seen walking around lately, you'll admit it's quite a problem. Or, for that matter, look at the person sitting next to you.

The population explosion is a universal dilemma that has been studied by leading demographers everywhere.

One solution to ease the situation is to force everyone to wear seersucker clothing. That would make room for ten more people per square mile all over the world. Of course, you may say the people at the South Pole wouldn't be comfortable in seersucker, but then, they can't expect us to solve *all* their problems for them.

Overcrowdedness is all a matter of geography. To a person living in the Arctic, living conditions in Manhattan, where there are one hundred and forty-five people per acre, would seem miserable. But, to a person living in Manhattan, living conditions don't seem miserable ... they *are* miserable.

Moving to another part of the world, let's take a look at Java. Here there are one thousand people per square mile. Needless to say, they marry quite young in Java.

As for the United States, the most crowded area

1	is the eastern seaboard region, where one hundred and
2	eighty people live in each square mile. This area includes
3	New York, New Jersey, Connecticut and the steam room
4	at the Americana Hotel.
5	Let's look at the birthrate sweepstakes in
6	Hollywood, which has an average 3.5 children per
7	marriage. And the average Hollywood citizen has an
8	average 3.5 marriages, so we see the trouble right off.
9	This is rather distressing news, but you may take
10	hope from the fact that people don't multiply anywhere
11	near the rate of the lowly amoeba. Just let this sink in:
12	in one week, an amoeba could produce enough offspring
13	to exceed the weight of the whole world, if given adequate
14	food and favorable circumstances. I can't outline the set-
15	up here, but I can tell you it includes soft lights and
16	bolero music.
17	But getting back to the human problem, how does
18	this population boom affect us financially? Bad. Bad! In
19	America, since the end of World War II, the birth rate
20	spiralled up to thirty per one thousand. That's babies,
21	gang. Now let's be practical. Think of the countless man-
22	hours spent away from the machines. At eight dollars
23	and fifty cents an hour, think of what this does to our
24	economy. Is it any wonder we've fallen behind in the
25	arms race?
26	Now what can we do to stem the tide? Here are
27	some suggestions offered by leading authorities: 1.
28	Famine. 2. World War III. 3. Spice-free diets. 4.
29	Compulsory exercise. 5. Draft Burt Reynolds. Think it
30	over. Thank you and goodnight. *(MONOLOGIST exits.)*
31	
32	
33	
34	
35	

#17

The Automatic Elevator

CAST: Monologist — male.

MONOLOGIST: *(He enters and addresses audience immediately.)* You know something that really bothers me? Automatic elevators. I miss the ones that had real uniformed people operating them. I mean, you always had someone to talk to, to reassure you, when you were trapped between floors.

But they've gone the way of the blacksmith, the doctor who makes house calls, the little girl who lives in the lane and the candlestick-maker. Undoubtedly, these swift, sleek automatic jobs save time and money — but they do pose certain problems for humanity.

For instance — what if the sign says, "This elevator holds one thousand, five hundred pounds," and the twelve people inside crowd together even tighter to make room for a fat person eating a candy bar?

What if the sign in the car says, "This elevator is inspected by . . ." and there's no one's name there. That'll heighten your fear quotient.

What if you're returning to your office with a cheese and garlic sandwich, and you get caught between floors in the elevator with a pretty girl you've been trying to make an impression on?

What if you're about to step into an automatic elevator and you notice the lobby desk captain selling flight insurance for passengers? Think about it.

What if the piped-in music plays a waltz when you're in a tango mood — and so is the pretty girl alone in there with you? What if the piped-in music *does* play a tango and you're in the car alone? Think about *that*!

What if the elevator begins dropping too quickly from the thirty-fifth floor and the piped-in music plays "How Deep is the Ocean?" That's got to make you tense.

About the only good thing I can see is that the automatic elevators are always there. They don't take vacations. Never grumble when they don't get a raise. They're never late for work. Never absent. *(Looks at watch.)* Pardon me. I have an appointment on the fiftieth floor and I'm a little late right now. *(MONOLOGIST walks off a bit. Looks at wall. Pretends there is a sign there and reads it. Repeats, reading sign.)* **Sorry. Awful headache. Won't be in today.** *(Does confused take to audience. Then he starts off slowly.)* **Well, if I could only find that girl dancer, I'd tango up the fifty flights.** *(Calls Offstage.)* **Oh, miss!** . . . *(He begins to tango as he exits, calling.)* **Miss, miss, come dance with me . . . come dance with me . . .** *(He tangos to his exit.)*

#18

Maniac-Killer

CAST: Monologist — male; aggressive, forceful, a police chief.

PROPS: Desk, phone, sheet of paper.

MONOLOGIST: Men, as your police chief, I tell you now that we must stop this outrageous crime spree. I'm talking about the maniac-killer. Last week alone, four maniacs were killed. And I'm on the spot.

This morning, I got a call from J. T. Frenzy, president of the Society of American Maniacs. "Chief Moran," he said — I interrupted to tell him my name was Chief Higgins — "Chief Moran," he continued, "our city streets aren't safe for maniacs to walk on anymore."

I'm getting it from both sides. I got this note earlier today. *(Takes out paper, reads.)* "Chief Higgins, I will kill you. I will get you alone and break your back and kick your teeth in and steal your gloves. I will burn down your house, ruin your car and bash in your skull with a blunt object.

"Send this letter to three friends. Do not break the chain or you will have bad luck."

Let's get back to the maniac-killer.

In an all-out effort to solve the case, I've brought in three hoodlums, all of whom have a reputation for disliking maniacs. I'll have them walk in under the spotlight for a lineup, and I want to ask you men to hold your applause until all the criminals have been introduced. *(MONOLOGIST looks and waits as three imaginary hoods walk on.)*

Leading off is Flim-Flam Banghart. Did I

pronounce that right? *(Listens.)* No? How do you pronounce it? *(Listens.)* Montague Quicksilver. I see. Montague is one of our better-known arsonists, specializing in warehouses, failing restaurants and tenements. Nice fellow . . . just don't ask him for a match. Next. *(Looks to another vacant spot.)*

Here we have Harrison Shugrue. He's here because he looks like a criminal. Look how close together those two eyes are. Of course, they're far away from the other eyes, but that in itself is a criminal characteristic. Next.

Last, but not least, wearing number seventeen, hailing from Boise, Idaho, the Oklahoma Kid, Penman Jones. Penman writes notes for a living, usually bomb hoaxes. Last month alone, he was responsible for my sending eighty-seven men out on fourteen wild goose chases. And we caught no wild gooses . . . er . . . geese. No wild geese. By the way, Penman — and this goes for all bomb scare note-writers who might hear of this talk — when you send a note saying you've planted a bomb somewhere, for heaven's sake, plant a bomb. Sending men out like that for nothing is just a waste of the taxpayers' money. Besides, you're setting a bad example for our youngsters. Step down. *(To audience)* Sergeant Mullaney, stand behind each of them, now, and hold your hand over their heads. Men, you applaud for the best suspect . . . and no whistling. *(MONOLOGIST can move about here. Audience, if invited, can do the applauding.)*

Let's hear it now for number one . . . *(Applause)* number two . . . *(Applause)* and number three . . . *(Applause)* And the winner . . . Penman Jones. Penman, register with the desk sergeant for the semi-finals. Can you come back next Thursday? Wonderful. Your opponent will be selected from the top three suspects of the Twenty-third Precinct, and I'm looking forward to an exciting contest.

(*Phone rings. MONOLOGIST picks it up and listens.*) What? You've kidnapped Mayor Grimseley? You're *Mrs.* Grimseley? And you'll kill him unless you get some ransom money. Why kill him? (*Repeats.*) A mercy killing to end the suffering. But he's not suffering. I see . . . *you're* suffering.

Forty thousand dollars? I don't have that kind of money. I'm only a police chief. But wait . . . I'll dredge it up. (*Listens, repeats.*) What's that? You want it delivered to you by an unmarked police officer? Hold on. (*Calls out.*) Undercover lady Schneider, we need an unmarked police officer. Has that rash cleared up? Great.

(*Into phone.*) Mrs. Grimseley? We'll be sending over a fine officer. Officer Jane Schneider. She'll have the forty thousand. How will you know her? Oh, she's average height, shapely in a policewoman sort of way, blond . . . and . . . she'll be wearing a gun. (*Gloating, he hangs up the phone, nods to audience and exits.*)

#19

Interesting New Yorkers

CAST: Monologist — male or female.

PROPS: Large photographs of men if available. (Note: New York isn't essential here. Monologist can turn it into any large city — Chicago, Los Angeles, Denver, etc.)

MONOLOGIST: New York has its share of interesting people. I'd like to introduce you to a few of them. Take a look. *(With each name, he or she should hold up a picture.)*
Martin Moss — slumlord of the year for the past three seasons, Martin is out to win the award for an unprecedented fourth time. Martin won the award hands down when judges discovered he was keeping eighty-seven illegal aliens in a one-room, cold-water, rat-infested, poorly ventilated flat and getting one hundred and ninety-seven dollars a month. His eventual goal is to crowd one hundred tenants into a reconverted garbage pail and get four hundred dollars a month. For his outstanding efforts to further dehumanize New York, Mr. Moss was presented with an autographed swamp rat.
Stretch Stritch, as he is known, stands seven feet, two inches tall, just two inches shorter than when he received a brutal beating in a Bronx amusement park and achieved fame as the "Tallest Mugging Victim" in the history of that borough. He was beset by a trio of hoodlums who worked him over thoroughly and forced him to walk across the nearby stream on a terrace of lily pads. He was further humiliated when a near-sighted midget mistook him for Mt. Rushmore and climbed him. Stretch has since withdrawn from public life and is now

living quietly in the New Hampshire Home For the Tall.

      Bill Booster — King Bill the First is the way people always referred to Bill Booster, who was the first New Yorker to try everything. The late Mr. Booster was the first to go through the Holland Tunnel, over the George Washington Bridge, into the Automat, under the Central Park Bridge, across the Staten Island Bay on the ferry and up to the top of the Empire State Building. He died when he became the first to try to walk across the Harlem River Bridge — he tried it three weeks before it was completed.

      Marlo Blank — Marlo was honored for contributing greatly in the city's efforts to relieve the crowded housing conditions. He rented out the vacant stare in his eyes. Thank you for your interest in interesting New Yorkers. *(MONOLOGIST exits.)*

#20

Disaster Films — Low-Budget-Style

CAST: Monologist — male or female.

PROPS: List that can be read from to aid the performer.

MONOLOGIST: Disaster. It's a recurring theme out in the land of Movieville. People screaming, dying . . . and those are the producers.

But those films are big-money jobs. What about the producers who operate on a shoestring? Well, I'm happy to say they're surviving. Here are a few of the low-budget films about to appear on your screen. Some notes now on various films in the making.

"Bring Me the Passenger List!" Described by associates as the type of guy who would bring noisemakers and funny hats to the "Donner Party," producer Rance Gusto created a who-shall-survive film about the crash of a Piper Cub, leaving fourteen tourist passengers stranded atop Mt. Rushmore. Details of the story line weren't available, but it can be noted that screen credits will be given to Acme Cutlery Company, Tidy-Clene Paper Napkins and Sweet Breath After-Dinner Mints.

"Shake" — "We can't afford a real earthquake," said producer Al Shimner, "but we've got a doozy of a tremor caused by seventy-five elephants who leap én masse off a brick wall after seeing a mouse. This will rattle the crockery right off your shelves. We don't have the budget to wire seats, but we've hired a batch of nervous midgets to sit on patrons' laps during the climactic scene. Preview cards show eighty percent favorable responses, fourteen engagement announcements and two quick marriages."

"Bugs, You Bet!" — A sympathetic look as our crawling friends describe how they confiscate a salt water taffy factory and eat the Atlantic City boardwalk. Big scene occurs when they overpower a wax replica of Clint Eastwood, float him into the Delaware River and use him to ferry their troops to their target. Itching powder in the popcorn and on the towels in the lavatories put the audience in the proper mood.

"Buried Alive At Fire Island" — A sudden sandstorm whips up and buries a batch of merry bathers up to their necks in sand. Played against a sprightly musical score, vivid flashbacks tell the sordid tales of the trapped individuals who describe their falls from grace and the societal rejection which led to their banishment to Fire Island. Audience involvement? Yes. A team of dancing ditchdiggers come in from time to time and toss wet sand down the backs of the theater audiences.

"Lips" — a demonic man-nibbling guppy creates havoc as it terrorizes a New England seaside resort at the height of the tourist season. For audience participation, Fissner Studios will have a team of unmarried ushers who will kiss viewers lightly, simulating guppy bites, corresponding to the action on the screen.

(Addressing audience) And there you have the outlook for the low-budget disaster film season. And I might advise you — if you go to see any of these films, believe me, it will be a disaster! (MONOLOGIST exits.)

#21

Real Estate Spoken Here

CAST: Monologist — male or female.

PROPS: Newspaper with lines written inside for the benefit of the performer who may have memory problems.

MONOLOGIST: *(Carrying rolled up or folded newspaper.)* **Real estate people have a language all their own. Philologists say it is somewhere between Swahili and Esperanto and twice as confusing.**

    For the benefit of you people who might be apartment-hunting, I'm here to help interpret what you might see in the papers. For instance — *(Begins to read from the paper.)*

    When you see the words private entrance — you know what that means? It means there's a hole in the ceiling with a rope ladder.

    (Reads) ***High Ceiling* — Also free throw lines and baskets at each end of the room. *Private Swimming Pool* — Don't get your hopes up. *Private swimming pool* means the basement leaks. *Room of unusual beauty* —The last tenant left a pin-up picture of Racquel Welch hanging in the closet. *Free television* — Definition — if you lean out the window far enough to see into the neighbor's living room. *Music in every room* — Don't be deceived. It means the hi-fi addict in 3B is hard of hearing. *Convenient to transportation* — Situated twenty feet off the runway at La Guardia Airport. *Louis the XIV furniture* — Be careful of this one. *Louis the XIV furniture* means on the fourteenth of last month, Louis Jones slipped out without paying, so they kept his couch. *Full***

1   *basement* — Definition — filled with matchbook covers,
2   garden hose and souvenirs from Coney Island. *Rock*
3   *Garden* — That means — that last avalanche didn't do
4   anyone any good, but why gripe?
5   I hope I've added to your educational
6   accumulation — or, more likely — made you worry a bit.
7   **Thank you.** *(MONOLOGIST exits.)*
8
9
10
11
12
13
14
15
16
17
18
19
20
21
22
23
24
25
26
27
28
29
30
31
32
33
34
35

1	**#22**
2	
3	## Miss Weirdo
4	
5	
6	*CAST:* Monologist — female.
7	
8	*PROPS:* Cards for Monologist to read from, any outlandish
9	garments Monologist chooses to wear, wacky hat, funny gown,
10	etc. Monologist reads from cards to get questions from people
11	who need her particular kind of help.
12	
13	**MONOLOGIST:** *(Reads from card.)* **"Dear Miss Weirdo. I have**
14	**been invited to a semi-formal affair. Is it all right if I**
15	**wear a strapless evening gown?" — B.L. It is not all right**
16	**to wear a strapless evening gown, sir!**
17	**"Dear Miss Weirdo — My son Benjoy is a slob. In**
18	**a restaurant, he tosses salad and splits peas and makes**
19	**mud pies in the succotash. Shall I admonish him with a**
20	**small diatribe?" — L.T. No, L.T., rebuke him with a big**
21	**stick.**
22	**"Dear Miss Weirdo — My husband, a resident**
23	**brain surgeon with an advertising agency, always passes**
24	**out at formal dinner parties due to overeating. When he**
25	**slumps, is it proper to leave him there or prop him back**
26	**up?" — Z.M. Dear Z.M. — It is bad manners to use your**
27	**fingers on a glutton. Just brush him aside with your salad**
28	**fork.**
29	**"Dear Miss Weirdo — I have a bad memory for**
30	**names. Can you suggest a system which might help me**
31	**to remember?" — T.A. Dear T.A. — Associate a nickname**
32	**which might apply to the person's appearance, such as**
33	**"Baldy" or "Dippermouth" or "Sloppy." I think that would**
34	**help you, Eagle Beak.**
35	**"Dear Miss Weirdo — My boy, Farley, is out of**

high school and wants to go to Football Tech. I want him
to attend Business Normal. When he doesn't get his way,
he screams, hurts people, and bites his relatives. All this
because he wants the school of his choice. What do you
think I should put him through?" — B.R. Put him
through? How about a plate glass window?

"Dear Miss Weirdo — I am twenty-nine years old
and hesitant. Should I marry a girl on a salary of seventy-
five dollars a week?" — L.M. Seventy-five dollars a week?
No — of course not! Wait until she gets a raise.

(Reads another card.) "How about a gownless
evening strap?" — B.L. *No!* Get out of here, B.L. *(Throws
card away. Reads another card.)* "Hi, B.L. again. Then what
would you like to see me in?" A double-breasted
straitjacket, you dum-dum. *(Shakes head in dismay. Reads.)*
"Dear Miss Weirdo, I am thirty-five years old and want
to elope with a man five years my junior. In fact, that's
what I call him — 'My Junior.' He is five feet eleven
inches, weighs one hundred and sixty-five pounds,
smokes a pipe and parts his hair in the middle. Shall I
elope?" — G.R. Dear G.R. — That "My Junior" is my
husband, and my advice to you is to keep your hands off
him if you value your life. *(Seething as she exits.)* Wait 'til
I get home . . . *wait* 'til I get home . . .

#23

Order in the Court

CAST: Monologist — male or female.

PROPS: Big, floppy hat, eye patch, oversized overcoat and possibly a basketball, table or desk.

MONOLOGIST: Not having played basketball since I was in short pants, I may be a trifle behind the times in keeping up with the latest news from the basketball scene, but I am well aware that the sport is having its share of difficulties.

Most of the problem seems to center around the punishment handed out to players who commit too many fouls.

Some factions think a point and a half should be scored for each converted foul shot, but this would entail too much complex bookkeeping.

Another group contends that a perpetual perpetrator of court misdemeanors should be placed in a penalty box for a short time as in hockey. They are against making the performer leave the game after committing more than the allotted number of fouls.

This group contends that fans come first, and if a player is ejected from a game, the fans are being cheated. This, they say, is tantamount to removing Raquel Welch from a movie for committing a few minor transgressions. I have a plan which might help restore order in the court game.

For instance, if Larry Bird of the Boston Celtics gets called for his sixth personal foul, he wouldn't be tossed out. Rather he would be forced to play with his shoelaces untied and wearing a big hat. Then the pressure would be on his coach, who would have to decide whether to remove Bird or let him play with loose shoes and floppy hat.

If the infraction was of a more serious nature, like rabbit-punching an opponent who was attempting a foul shot, then the player would be required to put a patch over his left eye *(Does so)* and wear a big overcoat for the remainder of the game. *(Slips into large overcoat.)*

Stiffer penalties commensurate in severity with the offenses could be invoked at the referee's discretion. These might include requiring a fractious forward to play with one hand firmly held between his teeth *(Demonstrates)* or making an aggressive guard tie one foot behind his back *(Puts foot behind back)* and hop around *(Hops)* for the remainder of the game.

Such punitive measures would strike a happy compromise. It would add color to the game and undoubtedly would sit well with the fans. Wouldn't you be thrilled to see your favorite hoopster sink one from thirty feet out while wearing an overcoat and an eye patch?

It's worth a try, anyway, sports fans. *(Now, wearing an eye patch, a big overcoat and a big floppy hat, he catches a basketball tossed from Offstage and, nodding in acknowledgement to the audience, he hops out.)*

The Memory of a Fish

CAST: Monologist — male or female.

PROPS: None.

MONOLOGIST: Did you see that item recently about a new mind-controlling drug that they've tried successfully on fish? It erases their memories. Well, I have to tell you that one of the goldfish they tried it on was my pet Herman. Boy. I'm telling you, his memory is *shot*! Can't remember a thing.

Now you may ask what a goldfish has to remember. And I ask you in turn, have you ever peeked into their bowls when they didn't know it? I leave the rest up to you.

But getting back to Herman, I've tried everything to restore his memory. I leaned into his tank and shouted, "Hey, Herman, remember Marie, the cute swimmer with the shapely fintails?" Nothing.

Or, "Hey, Herman, watch out, here comes Felix the Cat." Herman just sits there and looks away.

I even brought him to see his crippled mother — she has water on the knee — hoping that would bring his memory back. No luck.

I was going to do a frontal lobotomy on him with a salad fork, but no, he wouldn't hold still for that. He's got a strong mind. Small . . . but strong. He's a determined fish who knows where he's going. Doesn't know where he's been, of course, but he's a real battler.

Right now, I have him reading his diary and going through his scrapbook. Something has to work.

1   If it doesn't, well, we'll probably have to pack him
2 off to the old fish home.
3   Either that or a burial at sea, with full military
4 honors. Thank you, fish-lovers. *(MONOLOGIST exits.)*
5
6
7
8
9
10
11
12
13
14
15
16
17
18
19
20
21
22
23
24
25
26
27
28
29
30
31
32
33
34
35

#25

Little-Known Books

4
5

6   *CAST:*   Monologist — male or female.

7

8   *PROPS:*   Some books.

9

10   MONOLOGIST: Ladies and gentlemen, (you know what you
11   are) I'm here to talk about books. Now, everybody knows
12   about the best-sellers, gamy though they may be. I'm here
13   to talk about little-known tomes that may add to your
14   cultural storehouse. Here at my hand, I have a few little
15   books that may increase your intellectual quotient.

16   *(As he describes a book, he picks one up and holds it up*
17   *for the audience.)* This is *Sage Words from Down Under* by
18   Arthur Auckland. A collection of four hundred and
19   eighty-one terse sayings from the 18th century bushmen
20   of Australia. Nearly all can be applied explicitly and
21   succintly to everyday dealings in today's political, social
22   and business life. Some are funny. Price — thirty-nine
23   cents.

24   *The North-South Book of Kale Cooking. (Holds up*
25   *another book.)* This book by Edwin Glutton features 23,574
26   recipes for using kale in your kitchen. Ever tried kale
27   cookies? Or kale kumquats? You will when you read this
28   delightful book for gourmets. Countless other kale tricks
29   for only — seven dollars and thirty cents. Check it out.

30   *Stories for Filling-Station Attendants,* by Edgar
31   Primer — a riotously funny book filled with anecdotes of
32   special interest to gas-station workers, but fun for the
33   entire family. Included are the famous stories of the rich
34   woman who wanted three gallons and the orphan who
35   ran away from home to join a nation-wide oil can concern.

Only sixty cents; high-test, seventy-five cents.

New City, North Carolina, by Harry Beeches — a handsome twelve-by-nineteen-inch book of old New City. See fields of tobacco, revel on the dirty roads, the murky swamps and other landmarks that distinguish this grand old Carolina town. See the realistic color photograph of the city's telephone exchange and several exciting pictures of local eccentrics committing various acts of a stupid nature — nineteen cents — with an old paperback trade-in.

The Sea Shell, by Winfield Conch. When was the last time you read a definitive study on this subject? Well, this is the book. A pictorial feature depicting the world's most famous shells is sure to please. You'll read about the "Shell Heard Round the World," "Two Shells that Pass in the Night," "The Good Shell That's Hard to Find" — yes, and even the "Shell in Mrs. Murphy's Overalls," together with many others you've read about but really never understood. Only one dollar and eighty-eight cents.

Secret Conversations of Edward Peabody, by Marcel Dullin — daring, intimate and revealing conversations of one of America's most forgotten men. Many knew him, some even spoke to him. Most ignored him. His refusal to appear in the public eye and his disdain for notoriety paved the way for his secret talks with people who figured they knew him well. You'll love the sparks of genuine genius and depth in Peabody's talk with Timmy Biler after Timmy lost his skate key. Just three dollars and twenty-two cents. *(Holds up book.)* **Come in and browse — and buy!** *(Exits.)*

#26

Those Late Night World War II Movies

CAST: Monologist — male. Role requires some good sound effects and gestures by performer.

MONOLOGIST: **I don't know about you folks, but I've gotten to be a late night television movie buff. Can't get enough of those old films.**

You know, flicks like "Gidget Finds a Body — Hers."

And mysteries — "Charlie Chan and the Mystery of Seven Clues."

(Chinese accent.) **"Number one son, where did you find the clues?"**

"In the clues closet." Stuff like that.

But my favorite movies are those great World War II films. Now that was a war to write home about. No controversy. And exciting. Especially the films about the bomber pilots and their crews. Boy, those B-17s used to zoom out of the clouds and they come right into your living room.

(Holds arms out, wing-like, and makes heavy bomber motor sounds.) **Nothing bothers those guys. True-blue American. There's always one guy from Happy-Go-Lucky, Kansas and there's always one guy from Brooklyn.**

And if you notice, the crews in these movies are comprised of every ethnic group in the world. You name a country, there's one of them in the crew. Irish, Jewish, Italian, Pole. They're all there.

It's a must. Audience identification. In fact, one important bombing mission was delayed three days because they were one Lithuanian short.

1   Action. They're up there in the clouds and all that
2   ack-ack, flak and bric-a-brac, all flying around and
3   they're up there telling jokes. Cool.
4   "Hey, Hennessy, hear the one about the traveling
5   yo-yo salesman . . ."
6   "Remember the one about the fly swatter and the
7   insect? Well . . ."
8   But then — the enemy.
9   "Goldstein. There are two Messerschmidts at five
10   o'clock. Hold it. Make that five Messerschmidts at two
11   o'clock."
12   "Is that Eastern Standard Time?"
13   *(Harshly)* "Shoot the planes, shoot the planes."
14   *(Machine gun sounds and gestures.)*
15   *(Sound of failing motor of falling plane with gestures.)*
16   See what I mean? Nothing stops these guys. Fifty bombers
17   go out — *(Arms extended, bomber sound.)* and seventy-five
18   come back!
19   Now they're back on the ground in the ready room.
20   "Hey, Hennessy, hear the one about the traveling
21   yo-yo salesman . . ."
22   But then the general comes into the room. *(Arms*
23   *extended, bomber sound.)*
24   Yeah, he's impressive. The men snap to attention.
25   That general is something. Tall, handsome, alert, dynamic.
26   His chest is filled with Oak Leaf Clusters and maybe a little
27   frosting from the cake at the party last night. He speaks:
28   "At ease, men. You may smoke."
29   So they give the general a hotfoot. There's a lot of
30   that horseplay going on.
31   But the general doesn't think it's funny. He tells
32   them they can't go to the USO dance and sends them on
33   another bombing mission. But they don't care. A dance or
34   a   bombing   mission   is   all   the   same   to   them.
35

1	*(Looks upward.)* **And there they go — up into the darkness**
2	**of night.** *(Arms extended, bomber sound.)*
3	**However, something goes wrong and they end up**
4	**at the USO dance after all. There they dance with pretty**
5	**hostesses and tell jokes:**
6	*(Feminine voice)* **"Hey Hennessy, hear the one about**
7	**the traveling yo-yo salesman . . ."**
8	**But life can't be all fun and games so it's off on**
9	**that bombing mission.** *(Arms extended, bomber sounds.)*
10	**Just to show that Americans aren't invincible; one**
11	**of the planes has to go down. You always know the guy**
12	**who's going to get it. He's pilot of the bomber next to Our**
13	**Guys. And he's a nice guy.** *(Big smile.)* **Blond, clean-cut,**
14	**doesn't smoke, drink, curse or leave the top off the**
15	**toothpaste tube. And he has his own baby shoes on a**
16	**string around his neck. For luck. Bad luck.**
17	**Enemy planes shoot apart the whole left side of**
18	**Nice Guy's bomber.** *(Machine gun sounds, gestures.)* **But Nice**
19	**Guy doesn't believe in war. Doesn't fight back. Just turns**
20	**the other cheek. And so they shoot apart the whole** *right*
21	**side of his plane.** *(Machine gun sounds, gestures.)*
22	*(Alarm in voice.)* **"Captain, we're going down!"**
23	*(Deeper voice, calm.)* **"At ease, men. You may smoke."**
24	**But even that doesn't go any good. The plane goes**
25	**down.** *(Downward spiraling gesture and sounds of falling*
26	*plane.)*
27	**Now the tempo builds up. The biggest bombing**
28	**mission of the war is coming up. The general comes into**
29	**Ready Room.** *(Wings extended, bomber sounds.)*
30	**This time as a tribute to his fallen comrade he**
31	**wears a photo of Nice Guy's baby shoes around his neck.**
32	*(Stern voice.)* **"Men, this is it. The biggest bombing**
33	**mission. We're going to bomb Bremerhavenunder-**
34	**strasse.** *(Looks at paper and reads.)* **That's Bre-**
35	**merunderhavstrassenneur . . .** *(crumples paper.)* **We're**

gonna bomb Stuttgart. We're gonna get the Messerschmidts."

"You mean the airplane factory, general?"

"No, we're gonna get a lot of Schmidts. Gus, Otto, Emil, Wolfgang, that crowd."

"Oh . . . I get it. We're gonna get a whole Mess-a-Schmidts."

"You got it."

Much laughter follows this exchange. The humor among the men never stops.

And there they go. Leap into their planes. The pilots are singing: "Off we go . . ."

The co-pilots are singing . . . harmony. "Off we go . . ."

Nobody knows the rest of the words.

The sky is black with bombers. *(Arms extended, bomber sounds.)*

(Stern voice.) "Johnson, open the bomb bays."

"Where is it?"

"You're standing on it."

"Yessirrr . . . aaa . . ."

But they finish the bomb run and it's back to the base, where they look at the photographs they took. *(Spreads hands open in front of face, as if examining pictures.)*

Well, they missed their target, but they destroyed Copenhagen.

And so they're back in the ready room, kidding around, punching each other on their Good Conduct medals and the general walks in. *(Arms extended, bomber sound.)*

He brings good news and bad news. The good news is that Nice Guy is safe. The bad news is — the war is over.

Saddened, the men stop fooling around and drown their sorrows in ginger ale and Mom's home-made

1 blueberry muffins.
2   Ah, they just don't make movies like that any
3 more.
4   *(Shakes head sadly, then brightens up and looks off-*
5 *stage. Waves hand in air and starts off-stage, shouting.)* **"Hey,**
6 **Hennessy, hear the one about the traveling yo-yo**
7 **salesman . . ."**
8
9
10
11
12
13
14
15
16
17
18
19
20
21
22
23
24
25
26
27
28
29
30
31
32
33
34
35

#27

A Blind Date for Little Awesome Fannie

CAST: Announcer — male or female; Monologist — male. Think Bob Newhart for character identification.

SETTING: MONOLOGIST is seated, dialing a phone. He speaks into the phone. An imaginary FANNIE is seated nearby.

ANNOUNCER: People seem to have a strong desire to fix other people up with what is termed "blind dates."

      Larry, a friend of mine, went on a blind date engineered by Arny Dimler, and eventually married the girl. That was ten years ago.

      I bumped into Larry the other day, asked him about married life and mentioned that the union was brought about by Arny Dimler.

      "Guess when you see Arny you'll want to reciprocate," I said.

      "Reciprocate!" he shouted. "I want to *retaliate*."

      Well, you can't win 'em all. But bad endings probably won't occur when a blind date is set up by a friendly, bright, understanding man like Bob Havens, who is always willing to help out a fellow human.

MONOLOGIST: Eddie? *(He turns to his left and gives a big smile and OK sign to FANNIE.)* This is Bob. How's old Uncle Ben? *(Pause)* When are the services? Too late, huh. Well, next time. I mean for someone else. Look, Eddie, you sound like you need cheering up. How would you like to go on a great blind date? My cousin is in town for the weekend.

      Fannie. Right. Fannie. That's her name. Back home they call her Little Awesome Fannie. Awesome. Right. You bet.

1	Oh . . . *(Looks to his left.)* **reddish hair. Clear eyes.**
2	**You'll love the eyes. They speak volumes.**
3	**No, I don't know. She has unlisted measurements.**
4	**But I can tell you Hugh Heffner sends her mash notes.**
5	*(Away from FANNIE)* **Oh . . . she's about forty-six —**
6	**forty-seven . . . but she's very young looking. And very**
7	**friendly. Loves animals. Good sign, right.**
8	**She's got a dog. Calls him Stanley. She cares for**
9	**him even though he has a bark impediment.** *(Looks around,*
10	*hesitating.)* **Arf! Arf!** *(Annoyed)* **I said Arf! Arf!** *(Pauses)*
11	**Shouldn't laugh at the handicapped, Eddie. Sure it's a**
12	**funny bark, but dogs will be dogs, as street cleaners say.**
13	*(Pause)* **Yes . . . I guess some would say that, too.**
14	**Oh. Yes. She's an archeologist.** *(Repeats)* **You can**
15	**dig that. Good, Eddie. She loves guys with a sense of**
16	**humor.**
17	**No, she doesn't have her own place. Lives in a**
18	**giant mansion with an older man. Right. A lot older. Very**
19	**rich. She calls him Daddy. Daddy Morebucks. No, it's not**
20	**like that at all.**
21	**Well, what do you say for this weekend.** *(Listens.*
22	*Repeats.)* **You're getting married Saturday.** *(Pauses)* **How**
23	**about Sunday?**
24	**You've got a friend?** *(Turns to left and smiles at*
25	*FANNIE.)* **What's he like?** *(Listens)* **A mild-mannered**
26	**reporter. Kent Clark. He's outside in a phone booth**
27	**changing his clothes. He's what?**
28	**He changed into a what?** *(Listens)* **Cape and**
29	**leotard with a big S on the front?** *(Laughs, stifling it as well*
30	*as he can.)* **No, I'm not laughing. Hey, he's your friend.**
31	**Tonight?** *(Looks toward FANNIE.)* **OK for tonight?**
32	*(Into phone.)* **Eight-fifteen under the Biltmore clock.** *On*
33	*top* **of the Biltmore clock?**
34	**He can crash through a brick wall, is faster than**
35	**a speeding bullet and can leap tall buildings in a single**

bound? OK, OK. *(Shakes head in disbelief.)* **Eight-fifteen on top of the clock.** *(Hangs up phone, looks at FANNIE.)*

(Mumbles to himself.) **Brick wall ... speeding bullet ... tall buildings ... on *top* of the clock ...**

(Talks directly to FANNIE.) **Little Awesome, you better take Stanley along with you tonight — you may be in for a rough evening.**

#28

My Fun Trip to New York City

CAST: Monologist — male. (Monologist comes on in friendly fashion, casual.)

MONOLOGIST: *(To audience.)* **How many of you have ever been to New York?** *(Acknowledges response with a nod.)* **Well, I just got back from my first visit to New York — the Big Apple — Fun City.**

Really impressed me. So much so that I kept a diary of my day in New York City.

(Takes out notebook from pocket and reads from scripts inside it.) **Woke up in my hotel room at seven a.m. to the sound of birds coughing on my window ledge.**

7:15 — I listen to the morning news and weather report on my neighbor's radio — blasting through the thin walls.

7:20 — Took a nice fun hot shower which turned cold when the guy upstairs turned on *his* hot shower.

7:30 — Out the door and into the elevator. Pushed the "down" button which shot me up *(Gestures upward.)* **to the seventeenth floor, where eight French poodles got on for their morning walk.**

7:35 — Pushed "up" button which plummeted us right down to the first floor.

7:36 — Out onto the street to hail cab. Impossible. Got my Big Apple morning exercise chasing a bus which overran the bus stop because he was seven hours behind schedule.

8:00 — Onto the bus. Give the driver a ten-dollar bill and receive two hundred nickles in change *(Aside)* **along with some very loud, choice comments about my**

background.

    And then came the ride uptown.

    8:15 — Bus reached Thirty-Second Street.

    9:15 — Bus reached Thirty-Fifth Street.

    9:16 — Bus tumbles into Con Edison street repair excavation. Pedestrians gather to applaud and shout their approval.

    9:17 — The mayor shows up to pose for pictures with the trapped passengers.

    9:18 — The mayor declares the accident an official Fun City Happening.

    9:19 — At the request of the mayor, Luciano Pavarotti rushes over from the Metropolitan Opera House to sing three choruses of "It's a Hap, Hap Happy Day" while Radio City Rockettes serve coffee and doughnuts to the passengers stuck on the bus.

    9:30 — Reach Pan Am building where my uncle works for an insurance company.

    9:35 — Cross engineers' picket line and hear more remarks about my background.

    9:40 — Enter insurance office and have reunion with my uncle, and naturally, talk insurance.

    10:30 — Helicopter misses heliport on building's roof and makes unscheduled landing in the insurance company's waiting room.

    10:32 — The mayor arrives for pictures among the wreckage and Lionel Ritchie arrives to sing three choruses of "I Want to be Around to Pick Up the Pieces," while Radio City Rockettes serve coffee and doughnuts.

    10:50 — Leave office, head downtown for P.S. 197 to visit my grade school history teacher.

    10:55 — Hail a cab.

    12:55 — *Get* a cab.

    1:15 — Pass Twenty-Fifth Street where a clean-up block party, headed by the mayor is sweeping

Twenty-Fifth Street and pushing the dirt down to Twenty-Fourth Street.

2:00 — Stopped by police barrier who are on the scene where two rival pacifist groups are beating each other over the heads with peace signs. Billy Joel rushes in to quell the riot by singing "You Always Hurt the One You Love."

2:15 — Listen to cabbie tell how he punched his last passenger in the mouth for only tipping him a dollar.

3:00 — Reach teacher's school — tip cabbie fifty cents.

3:02 — Phone my uncle. Ask if I'm covered for a punch in the mouth by a cabbie.

3:05 — Try to enter school. Cross picket lines of angry mothers; cross picket lines of angry children, cross picket line of angry teachers to find a smiling mayor being interviewed by Jim Jensen, *(Or Jane Pauley, Ted Koppel)* on TV. The mayor is explaining the strike. "Yes, this is a strike. See the strike? They are picketing. See them picket? They like to picket. This is a fun strike."

4:05 — Wave to history teacher on picket line and grab cab uptown. Pass Twenty-Fourth Street where clean-up block party is sweeping Twenty-Fourth Street and pushing dirt back on Twenty-Fifth Street.

5:00 — Go to dinner at a smart new restaurant — The Elegant Iconoclast. Wait for table.

6:00 — Get the table.

7:00 — Spot the waiter.

8:00 — Get check for $18.75. *(Aside)* I was short of cash so I gave him a $25 savings bond. He said what about my tip. I said wait ten years, you'll have a twenty-five percent tip coming.

8:05 — Call my uncle to see if I'm covered for being ... *(Aside to audience.)* well ... you know ... *(Might hold jaw.)*

    8:15 — Take an armored taxi for a fun evening of Shakespeare-in-Central Park.

    8:40 — Arrive Central Park. Cross Senior Citizens' picket line. Cross Black Power picket line. Cross White Power picket line. Cross Hispanic Power picket line. Cross Gay Power picket line. Cross Italo-American Power picket line. Cross Bulgarian Power picket line. Hear many more remarks about my background in five different languages.

    9:00 — Watch the mayor and city councilmen play Shakespeare on stage. *(To audience.)* Name of the play? "Much Ado About Nothing."

    11:30 — Back to my hotel. Take a quick look up and down hallway for muggers. Spot the same eight poodles coming out of elevator. Walk up to my room. Cross the hotel employees picket line outside my room. Hear more . . . *(Aside, nodding.)* you know . . . Go to bed listening to the Tonight Show on my neighbor's TV, Mel Tillis *(Any other singer.)* singing "Bluebird of Happiness."

    1:30 — Awakened by a National Guard parade. Open window and watch entire National Guard marching band topple into Con Edison excavation without missing a beat.

    4:45 — Finally lulled to sleep by the sweet sound of a garbage truck grinding up a row of double-parked cars.

    (Closes diary and puts it away.) A perfect end to a fun-filled day in Fun City.

#29

Whatever Happened To . . .?

CAST: Announcer — male or female; Monologist — preferably
female. (Emmaline)

SETTING: EMMALINE can be dressed in any comfortable manner
as she becomes your typical TV feature commentator. She can
be seated at a desk or standing. She can read the information
from the script or not, whatever the performer feels is best for
her.

ANNOUNCER: Nostalgia, yes folks, that's big today. You find
it everywhere. Books, television and radio shows,
sports magazines . . . newspaper articles . . . everywhere.
"Whatever happened to" is the key phrase here. And so,
to keep you up-to-date on some of our lesser known
celebrities of the past and what they're doing
now . . . here is Emmaline Hoskins.

EMMALINE: All show business fans will recognize the name
Esther Credenze. She was the woman who was sawed in
half on stage a thousand times. Lean, likeable Esther's
curly brown hair topped the smiling face that stuck out
of a long box and smiled at countless audiences as her
husband proceeded to saw her down the middle.
Audiences the world over gasped as they saw the trick
performed.

Unfortunately, Esther served as inspiration to
dozens of husbands throughout the nation who also
wanted to saw their wives in half in the worse way — and
proceeded to do so with the expected disastrous results.

Eventually the trick was banned on show
business stages. Notoriety forced Esther to quit.

But now — we ask — whatever happened to Esther Credenze, the lady who was sawed in half on stage?

We're happy to report that Esther is retired and is living quietly in Denver . . . and in New Orleans.

And how about Bertha Roundtree, World's Fattest Lady? Bertha as you no doubt remember, appeared on the Palace stage four times, forcing it to collapse under her weight each time. Who will ever forget the time she stumbled, fell and rolled the length of West Forty-Sixth Street, demolishing a parking lot, a delicatessen and three office buildings?

Well, after the depression, the world lost interest in female fat and so her career came to an end. As did many performers. Bertha went to Hollywood to work in films.

So, whatever happened to Bertha Roundtree?

Today, Bertha Roundtree, the world's fattest lady, works frequently as an actress. They dress her in a Matterhorn suit and she doubles as a mountain in low-budget documentaries.

Remember Farley Flambeau, the world's top-ranking fire-eater? He once ate seven pieces of flaming coal, a half-dozen biscuits baked by his new bride, and a fistful of blazing shish-ke-bab topped off with an order of cherries jubilee before going on stage to perform.

The heat was too much. Dozens in the audience fainted as he shoved red-hot pieces of coal into his mouth. Farley burst into flame.

Fortunately, members of his fan club, a group of volunteer firemen, leaped on stage and doused him. Shaken by his close call, Farley never performed again on stage.

But where is Farley Flambeau today? Whatever

happened to the world's number one fire-eater?

Well, happy to relate, he's doing all right. Farley Flambeau makes a good living as an oven in a Times Square pizza parlor.

Now we come to Nick Short, midget extraordinaire. Inch for inch, Nick Short was one of the most famous men in the world. Billed as the "Man who was so short he had to climb a ladder to tip his hat," Nick appeared in countless revues, stage acts and Broadway plays.

When the midget phase passed, Nick became a spokesman for a famous manufacturer of economy-size cars. His natty, tiny figure was a familiar sight popping in and out of small, compact cars on television and at conventions.

Then — one day in Los Angeles, he happened to be taking a shower when an earthquake hit. The first tremor hit and shot Nick through the air, causing his skull to get caught in the shower head.

A security guard came in, grabbed the tiny three-footer's ankles and tugged and tugged and tugged until he finally freed the entrapped Nick Short.

Today, Nick Short, once the world's most successful midget, is five-foot-ten and out of a job.

Thanks for listening, nostalgia buffs everywhere.

#30

Gossip Through The Ages

CAST: Announcer — male or female; Monologist — female. (Rhoda Raillery.)

SETTING: Desk with paper atop it. RHODA is seated, smiles at the audience. She's smart, tough, knowing. She's "today."

ANNOUNCER: Journalism — both print and verbal — takes many forms. Right now, the hottest trend seems to be gossip, good old plain back-fence gossip.

Dignified newspapers carry columns of juicy tidbits about their not-so-dignified readers, government officials and celebrities. Magazines are loaded with hot items about people in the news who leave each other, get into fist fights at Hollywood clubs and storm out of press conferences.

True, gossip is at its peak right now. But people have been gossiping and listening to speculative comments for years and years.

Our gossip expert has taken the trouble to dig out the items which amused, titilated and entertained people throughout the ages. The stories and opinions you will hear will appear in the soon-to-be published Anthology of Gossip.

And now, well-known gossip commentator, Rhoda Raillery.

RHODA: Hi, listeners. *(Glances down from time to time to get the items.)* There's no truth to the rumor Judge Crater is missing. Aside to Hannibal. Are you kidding? Elephants? Tunesmith Francis Scott Key has penned a little ditty called the "Star Spangled Banner." What's with the

1   high notes, Franny baby? People are starting to talk.

2   Court insiders are whispering that Marie
3 Antoinette has lost her head over some French nobleman.

4   We hear that General U.S. Grant is going souse
5 for the winter. *(?????)*

6   What's that they're saying about Carrie Nation?

7   Boston Harbor was the scene of quite a party.
8 They claim nothing but tea was served. However, I can
9 tell you that some of those guys were acting like wild
10 Indians. *(?????)*

11   Medics have advised Socrates to lay off the
12 hemlock.

13   Scotch those rumors you've heard elsewhere or
14 picked up from questionable sources about the so-called
15 feud between Aaron Burr and Alexander Hamilton.
16 They're buddies. In fact, they're meeting each other
17 tomorrow at dawn in Fort Lee, New Jersey.

18   Dip your pen in sunshine and write a "get well"
19 card to General Custer.

20   Was Thomas Edison lucky? Just asking.

21   What's that they're saying about Thomas
22 Jefferson?

23   Meanest thief in the world — the fellow who stole
24 George Washington's wooden teeth at a recent
25 convention.

26   Big shindig at Dracula's Mortuary Room the other
27 p.m. He threw a big "come as you were" party.

28   What's that they're saying about Carrie Nation,
29 Thomas Jefferson and George Washington's teeth?

30   We don't like what's going on in Massachusetts.
31 We've met Lizzie Borden and she's a nice kid. Rumor-
32 mongering can hurt the career of this winsome little
33 charmer who's carving out quite a name for herself in
34 the New England tree-chopping tourney.

35   Hippocrates, a Greek medic, claims to have

discovered the cure for the common scold.

Silent screen star Rita Van Boom has been happily married for thirty-three years — to nine different men.

Someone stole Peter Stuyvesant's wooden leg and made him hopping mad.

If you have a free moment or two, catch Lady Godiva's equestrienne bit at Coventry. A real winner. No cover, no minimum. Shows at two, four and seven-thirty and whenever the wind blows.

And . . . *(Looks at audience with sly smile.)* what's that they're saying *(Gestures toward audience.)* about that man in the second row?

And that's the world of gossip down through the years up to today.

Thank you. *(Curtain or blackout.)*

#31

And Now, Coming to You Live . . .

CAST: Announcer — male or female; Monologist — male.

ANNOUNCER: If you've been watching TV lately, you may have noticed a few bits of casting that may seem out of place. For instance, you have a 250-pound Chicago Bear fullback and a TV news analyst on game shows and, as one critic said, "who knows we may soon see a pro-basketball star doing a two-step on a Saturday morning kiddy's show, or a member of the President's cabinet doing a comedy routine on Sunday's Sports Spectacular."

Well, anything to hypo the ratings, right? But imagine if an ex-sport's great was assigned to do a live, on-the-spot bit of news coverage. With that thought in mind, let us present Big Bill Barrett, live, and on the scene . . . *(MONOLOGIST enters, carrying a mike.)*

MONOLOGIST: Hi, viewers. This is Big Bill Barrett talking to you from Broadway and 234th Street where a man has landed after his stove blew up, sending him flying 145 feet, nine inches through the air — a new national record for the event.

Golly, there's a good turnout here today. Maybe five hundred spectators looking on against a colorful background of firemen working feverishly to extinguish the blaze in what had been this man's residence.

Some nurses and paramedics are working on the man . . . *(Calling off.)* Hey, you, take that big black thing from the guy's face . . . how'm I supposed to talk to him? We're on TV. Right . . . The man's name is Ed LeBrenner. Remember that name, sports fans.

OK, doc . . . back off, you're blocking me.

(Brings mike down to floor level.) **Mr. LeBrenner, are you OK? How do you feel? Tap twice if you hear me. Oh, he's nodding, folks. Tell me, Mr. LeBrenner, how does it feel to be the holder of the new record for being blown through the air by a stove explosion?**

What's that? You're proud. And rightfully so. I notice you're lying there in what seems to be considerable pain. Does it hurt? *(Pause)* **Only when you preen. I see. Well, hardiness is a lasting virtue and especially welcome in this day and age. Tell me, were you thinking world's record when you started out on your epic flight?**

(Pause, listening.) **When you passed Mrs. Krasnit's second-story window you knew you had a chance. Gotcha. I know accident and sports fans alike will be interested in this. What did you think about while making your historic trip?**

(Pause, listening.) **You wondered if you stopped a sneeze half-way through would you be entitled to a full "God bless you." Yes ... I see. Wonderfully spiritual and uplifting — in a way. I guess.**

(Looking off.) **Nurse ... get that funny looking thing off his face. How do you expect the viewers to see his face?**

(Back to victim.) **Any other thoughts?**

(Pause, listening.) **You thought of making pre-stained sweatshirts for unathletic guys who want to make out they're athletes. Sure. Bolstering the egos of under-achievers. Great. Noble thought. You're a sportsman and a credit to your race. By the way, what is your race?**

(Pause, listening.) **Half-mile low hurdles — while holding a sixteen-pound shot. Golly, that's got to inspire hope in any person, handicapped or not. LeBrenner, despite your near tragedy and while you're lying there racked with hideous pain, you're in wonderful spirits. Why?**

1   *(Pause, listening.)* **It's the first time you've been out**
2   **of the house without your wife in twenty-five years. Mr.**
3   **LeBrenner, that's an old joke.**
4   *(Pause, listening.)* **So is your wife.** *(Looking away,*
5   *shaking head.)* **OK, doc, drag him out of there. Tune in**
6   **again tomorrow, live action fans, when we will present**
7   **live, from Times Square, a genuine full-length mugging**
8   **performed by two consenting adults. Goodnight, sports**
9   **lovers everywhere.**
10
11
12
13
14
15
16
17
18
19
20
21
22
23
24
25
26
27
28
29
30
31
32
33
34
35

Dear Gabby's Advice to Prisoners

CAST: Announcer – male or female; Monologist – female. (Gabby)

SETTING: Desk, script or cards for MONOLOGIST to read from at desk.

ANNOUNCER: We've all read those advice columns in the papers aimed at people who are emotionally distraught, advice for party-givers, advice for people who want to repair their homes, advice to the loveworn ... er ... lovelorn ... but no one seems to care about offering sage advice to our nation's most rapidly growing segment — prisoners. The incarcerated. That is, until Dear Gabby's column. Meet Dear Gabby. *(GABBY either enters and sits at desk or is seated there during the ANNOUNCER'S opening spiel.)*

GABBY: *(Reads)* Dear Gabby: What is your favorite prison newspaper? Signed, Journalism Buff.

Dear Journalism Buff: My favorite is the Sing Sing Sentinel. It covers all the inside stuff and has an excellent travel section with recommended getaway routes outlined in red.

(Reads) Dear Gabby: Since I've been in jail I miss my favorite food — strawberries. Why won't the warden serve me strawberries? Signed: Gourmet.

Dear Gourmet: The warden won't serve you strawberries because he's afraid you might break out.

(Reads) Dear Gabby: None of your corny strawberry gags when you answer my question or you'll get yours when I get out. Now listen up. My wife plans to bake me a cake with a file in it. Any recipe tips?

Signed — Angry Gourmet.

Dear Angry Gourmet: I know your wife and she's a rotten cook. Tell her to bring you a chain saw so you can cut the cake and get the file.

(Reads) Dear Gabby: My cellmate drives me nuts playing solitaire all night long. How can I get even? Signed — Revenge Seeker.

Dear Revenge Seeker: Play a game yourself — blackjack. Take a blackjack and whack his skull until he's not playing with a full deck.

(Reads) Dear Gabby: I'm outta here in two weeks. I have a contract for a hit in a crowded restaurant. I know it's an etiquette dilemma. Any suggestions? Signed: Socially Aware.

Dear Socially Aware: Order food to cover up the sound of the pistol shot. Celery, radishes, cereal that pops and, of course . . . a Maxim silencer. You never want to disturb other diners.

(Reads) Dear Gabby: How can I become a trusty? Signed — Ambitious.

Dear Ambitious: Shoot another trusty.

(Reads) Dear Gabby: I'm here at Joliet. They got me on trumped-up charges of wiping out an entire factory softball team, with my wife. We want to be transferred. Where do you suggest? Signed: The Friendly Duo.

Dear Friendly Duo: Why not request the Walled-off Astoria? They have a friendly staff, fine food and an electric chair that seats two.

(Reads) Dear Gabby: I love to read. The warden says I can't have Barbara Cartland or any other novels by other romance writers. Why not? Signed: Avid Reader.

Dear Avid: You can't read that type of book because it is escape literature.

(Reads) Dear Gabby: My fellow prisoners shout out numbers like twenty-six and forty-nine from their cell blocks every night after supper and then they all break out in laughter. My cellmate said they have been here so long they need jokes for their morale. They don't waste time telling them completely, so they just shout out the numbers of the jokes. And you should hear them laugh! I tried it. I called out seventy-four. No one laughed. Why? Signed: Humorless.

Dear Humorless: Maybe it was just the way you told it.

(Reads) Dear Gabby: I've been in prison sixty-five years and they're starting something called conjugal visits. What does this mean? Signed — Larry.

Dear Larry: Sixty-five years? Means nothing to you!

We leave you on that note with a reminder that my latest book is entitled "For He's a Jolly Good Felon." Buy it if you choose. This is not a *Hard Cell*. We see by the calendar on the wall it's time to say to all of you: "If you think you deserve a good break — go ahead and make one."

#33

Meet David Punkrock

CAST: Announcer — male or female; David Punkrock — star, legend in his own mind, and in the mind of the enthusiastic announcer.

ANNOUNCER: David Punkrock — he walks like a giant in a cabbage patch of musical midgets, his guitar strung jauntily between his knees, making strides difficult, representing the misrepresentation presented by those who present and those who deceive, corrupt, whinny and negate the honest, true values in the never-never land of the melodic spasms that divest and divide, crash and collide but serve to keep the youth culture on the beaten kick.

He sings, his vibrato trembling with uvulistic virtuosity, as he tweaks his gilt-encrusted lapels and wraps himself coyly around his latest gold-star million-sales record which has given him two $80,000 cars, undershirts that smile and ripple and homes in three countries. All of these things he rejects spiritually and emotionally, but enjoys to the hilt to avoid the pejorative tag of hypocrite. But now — meet DAVID PUNKROCK!

(DAVID enters the scene. He is outfitted in a garish, almost electric costume, his collar askew, tie draped over his shoulder, sleeves ripped, jacket coming almost to his knees and shoes of different colors. He addresses the audience with arrogance and complete lack of concern for them. He is all for DAVID PUNKROCK. He holds his guitar, dangling on a cord tied around his neck. You've seen this type of airhead — complete — right to the punk-style hairdo, numerous times before.)

DAVID: What it is is a bigger-than-life space, a set-up of the far-flung and in-between. *(He occasionally twangs the guitar to emphasize a point.)* **The moguls who preside over the wax industry with the so-called revolutions-per-minute crowd buy us, own us, sell us for what they get, bartering us for gold and keeping their own shiny suits and narrow pudgy faces cluttered with greed counting the coin we give them through our artistic excellence and mournful visages.**

The bit about 'getting high with the help of my friends' is the only answer and don't listen to no elected public official because they get elected by funny people over thirty who watch the boob tube alla time until lights flicker off in their shallow minds and they tremble with fright, afraid to allow freedom to the people who count when the scene is ripe and willing.

When they lower the voting age to nine we'll have true elections. Honesty, that's what youngsters have, untainted by greed and the commuting train and those luxurious high-rise kiosks which encompass mankind and kill folks, is all.

You get locked in with the standards and you become one of the mob of faceless cretins. I mean it's *they* and *us*. *Us* and *they*. *They* and *them*. *Us* and *we*. *We* and *this*. *This* and *us*. *Us* and *them*. It's all got to come to a mind-blowing climacteric which is the inconsequential hangup thrust upon us by the elderly and senile who are in charge. I said: *Who are in charge!*

We've got the power and free-wheeling synergetics bushing us from behind and the carrot of confrontation teasing us from the the front and if that ain't enough to get you off your duff and into the syndicate of joy, then you ain't ever going to be with it!

Legalize everything!

And I must admit straight out now that we're going through a musical comedown because of the apathetic nihilism coursing through us. Where are the Spiteful Aborigines who ground their way into our hearts on the Violence label? Where are the Spit Benders? How about the Rotund Confession? The Electric Armpit? The Fat Lady?

Bummers come and bummers go, but tripsters and hipsters never say the word for mankind because we're all one. I'm you. You're me. I'm them. They're us. We're them. And we're all John Phillip Sousa and don't forget it.

I like the smell of leather but don't call me a cop-lover. I don't believe in the No-Knock Law and I'm against frisking, unless it's done by two consenting adults.

Laws restrict. Prisons confine. Let us all float free. After all, what harm is visionary images of truth? Distortion is the bread of life.

Dig it heavy, baby. Ha-ha-ha. Laugh that off, world!

That is if you haven't forgotten how to laugh! *(He sneers and stares with intense dislike at the audience. He strums his guitar savagely and strides off with a swagger. ANNOUNCER returns, looks after DAVID as he exits.)*

ANNOUNCER: Yes, David Punkrock. He walks big and high with mighty strides across the barren land, his guitar strung jauntily between his knees, his chin set defiantly between his guitar and his knees set nattily between his chin.

(Intoning, seriously, meaningfully.) **Espresta accapella rubato sic transit mundanis, ad nauseum, David Punkrock.** *(CURTAIN or BLACKOUT.)*

#34

Understanding Those Football Referees

CAST: Announcer — preferably male; Monologist — female.

ANNOUNCER: Women have been making inroads into previously all-male sports. We have female softball players, female footballers, wrestlers, boxers and weight lifters. We also have had basketball referees of the feminine persuasion, baseball umpires and yes, even lady football officials, such as Nancy Charmaine, college football referee and head of the Call Them Like They Are Gridiron Official School for Girls. Nancy? *(NANCY comes out in a typical black-and-white striped jersey and all-white official slacks. She looks down at her outfit.)*

MONOLOGIST: Have you ever seen such a tacky get-up? Ugh . . . but enough about fashion. You people are here to become football officials and naturally you have to know what our signals are and what they mean. Watch and listen. We'll start off with the simple ones.

(Stands with hands on hips.) **Offside — five yards.**

(She wriggles as she walks a few steps.) **Backfield in motion — penalty five yards.**

(She goes through kicking motion.) **Kicking an object other than the ball — ten yards.**

You have to watch out for this one. *(Comes down with vicious over-hand motion.)*

Use of hammer more than six inches long — penalty: half the distance to goal — or to Chicago, whichever is closer.

(Puffs out cheeks, bloats out stomach and pats belly.) **Too much time at the refreshment stand. Penalty, ten days at your local Weight Watchers Club.**

1	*(Hands in front, rotates hands in rolling motion.)*
2	**Attention Coach** *(Name of local or rival coach.)*, **your car's**
3	**brakes gave way; it's rolling down the hill toward the**
4	**stadium wall.**
5	*(Cringes, holds hands over ears.)* **Forget it, coach.**
6	*(Grimaces, makes ugly face.)* **Extreme ugliness**
7	**without the face mask — ten days in the dog pound.**
8	*(Goes into an exaggerated strut.)* **Illegal procedure —**
9	**three days on bread and water.**
10	*(Arms extended, looks skyward.)* **Very serious**
11	**injury — time out.**
12	*(Hands clasped, eyes closed, she falls to her knees.)* **Very**
13	**serious injury — don't send flowers. Please send**
14	**contributions to the School for Delinquent Linebackers.**
15	*(Quick passing motion with right hand.)* **Roughing the**
16	**passer — ten yards.**
17	*(Slashing motion with palm behind kicking right knee.)*
18	**Roughing the kicker — twenty yards.**
19	*(Shocked look, sudden motion as if hitting someone in*
20	*the face.)* **Roughing the cheerleader — thirty days in**
21	**solitary confinement.**
22	**Well, those are the main signals you have to know.**
23	**Some hints: Get to know the team members. Remember,**
24	**a good official and a good player go hand-in-hand — but**
25	**not on the playing field.**
26	**Be impartial — no matter how cute that**
27	**quarterback may be.**
28	**And, most important — learn to know all the rules**
29	**and terminology of the game.** *(Starts off, turns, raising both*
30	*hands high overhead, the touchdown signal.)*
31	*(Shouting off-stage.)* **Go to it, boys. Hope both teams**
32	**score plenty of Home Runs!** *(Exits)*
33	
34	
35	

#35

Vicarious Vacations

CAST: Announcer — male or female; Monologist — male or female.

ANNOUNCER: A little frightened to fly overseas on your vacation because of those terrorists who might hi-jack your plane? A little leery about taking your vacation in one of America's large cities because of those terrorists who gather around your car stopped at a red light and stay there until you give them money to wipe your windshield with a dirty rag?

 Well, many people are. Travel agents report a sharp decline in business.

 But on hand to remedy that situation, is the well-known entrepeneur and innovator Ed *(Edwina)* Spencer, founder of Vicarious Vacations. Mr. *(Miss)* Spencer...

 (MONOLOGIST comes on stage. He can either sit down or stand.)

MONOLOGIST: Yes, why risk life and limb and money belt traveling abroad or chancing it in a big city. Why not stay at home and enjoy your vacation? Vicarious Vacations brings your vacation home to you.

 Now you can stay home and enjoy — *(He/she might hold up large printed signs with the names of the various cities as he describes them.)*

 PHILADELPHIA — Simulated weekend for two in a Philadelphia hotel. Vacation kit includes sleeping pills, ear plugs and a TV schedule in which the late, late show comes on at 8:30 p.m.

 We will include a mockup of a lethargic bellboy and a sleepy room clerk who won't even raise an eyebrow when you sign in under the name of William Penn,

1	Benjamin Franklin, Mrs. Benjamin Franklin and yes,
2	even Chubby Checker.
3	Price for this slowed-down, laid-back vacation —
4	a mere $32.50. This includes a plate of Philadelphia
5	scrapple and an autographed photo of famed
6	Philadelphia manager Connie Mack, and a video tape
7	depicting a team of maladroit workmen trying to repair
8	the Liberty Bell.
9	MIAMI BEACH — Sit back in your living room and
10	enjoy a fabulous vacation in the land of sun and fun.
11	Our Miami-trained crew will descend upon your
12	home some evening without your knowledge and dump
13	in thousands of live reptiles, crawling things and many
14	other slithering reptile-type objects which will keep you
15	hopping — Miami-style.
16	On Saturday night, a tall waitress in an
17	abbreviated costume will drop in, serve you a watered-
18	down ginger ale, charge you $7.50, smile and leave as fast
19	as she came.
20	We will also tamper with your sun bathing
21	machine so you will be burned to a crisp, requiring the
22	attention of a reliable doctor. Your friends will envy you!
23	Price of $89.90 also entitles you to an alphabetized
24	list of Miami's water-logged swimmers and a crushed
25	beach chair once used by Jackie Gleason.
26	NEW YORK CITY — Don't forget little old New
27	York even if you're from the wilds of North Dakota. For
28	just a teensy sum you can enjoy New York without leaving
29	your home.
30	Kit includes — seven shirt collars covered with
31	pollution from genuine bus exhaust.
32	Twenty-seven pounds of garbage from one of the
33	Big Apple's nicer neighborhoods picked up during the
34	city's recent garbage strike.
35	A sixteen-millimeter movie showing a parade of

slumlords marching to martial strains supplied by the Hard Core Unemployable Marching Band.

Price — a low, low $104.45.

If you act quickly, a crack team of New York street repair men will come to your very own street, rip it up in ten minutes flat and disappear forever. Go New York today!

AFRICA — A measly two-hundred dollars will buy you the thrill of a lifetime — a simulated trip to darkest Africa. For that low, low price, we lock you in a steam room with a disturbed rhinocerous and give you a rubber plant and a machete.

For an extra twenty dollars we give you an eight-by-ten glossy photo of a cowardly gun bearer together with the symptoms of a mysterious jungle fever.

For quick action on this once-in-a-lifetime offer, we will send you full-size vinyl replicas of Maureen O'Sullivan and Johnny Weismuller in leopard-skin outfits and will include, at no extra cost, an escape route written in code on the head of a pygmy.

ITALY — Let Vicarious Vacations take you to Italy without letting you leave your easy chair.

Venice? Why, of course. For this part of the trip we recreate the waterways of Venice by sending you an inflatable kayak and have a team of trained plumbers come in to stop up your drains so your water pipes back up into your living room.

You've heard of the famous 'Three Coins in the Fountain' tradition in Rome? For that, we substitute twenty-seven macaroni wafers and a giant vat of marinara sauce.

Also included is an aerial photo of Sophia Loren and, if at all possible, you will be granted an audience with Jerry Vale.

Price — $225. Slightly higher west of Papa Gino's

1	Pizza Parlor.
2	SOUTH SEAS TROPICAL ISLAND PARADISE —
3	Everyone has dreamed of spending a vacation in the
4	South Seas, lying under the sun on a tropical island, and
5	letting your cares and worries drift out into the blue
6	Pacific.
7	Well, here's your chance. A group of specially
8	trained vandals will destroy your home's heating system
9	so that your house maintains a constant temperature of
10	108. Naturally, we nail shut the windows and doors and
11	punch holes in the roof for that occasional rainstorm
12	you'll enjoy.
13	We supply you with a pet monkey named Chee-
14	chee who will throw coconuts at you when you least
15	expect it.
16	As a special bonus for you buyers who act fast,
17	we offer our Tidal Wave Special. This is what really makes
18	you feel you're right on that magic tropical island. What
19	we do is weaken the foundations of your home, flood the
20	area and actually wash your house right out of sight.
21	Price $650. Tidal Wave Special requires payment
22	in advance.
23	Yes, let Vicarious Vacations take you for a ride.
24	Our motto: "Stay Now — Pay Now."
25	
26	
27	
28	
29	
30	
31	
32	
33	
34	
35	

#36

The Car Accident

CAST: Announcer — male or female; Monologist — male. (Bob Newhart for character identification.)

SETTING: Chair in the center of stage. If curtain is used, ANNOUNCER talks in front of it. It would then be opened to reveal MONOLOGIST seated in the chair.

ANNOUNCER: **According to the latest highway accident figures, it would seem American motorists spend a good deal of their time asking to see each others' licenses and having fender dents hammered out.**

If you haven't had an accident yet, remember the most important factor is: stay calm. And try to stay in your own seat — after the crash.

A friend of mine, Montmorency, is cool and calm. As an automobile driver he's considered an ace — five accidents, with two probables.

Here's what happened on his most recent outing. It was a fine sunny Sunday afternoon. He was driving upstate, enjoying the country scenery when it happened. He was belted right in the middle by another car crossing the intersection without stopping.

Here's how cool, calm Montmorency reacted when the other driver came over to the car.

MONOLOGIST: *(Seated in chair.)* **Yes, sir, seems we did have a little bang-bang.** *(Listens, repeats.)* **Oh, you were a kamikaze pilot during the war.** *After* **the war?**

Any damage to your car? *(Repeats)* **The chrome was knocked off the ashtray and . . . and you're suing me.**

My car got hit a bit too. I mean the windshield

1	wiper used to be on the *outside.*
2	And look at the way the whole car is bent like a
3	big "U". *(Repeats)* Perfect for making U-turns. That's
4	funny. Glad to see you keep your sense of humor despite
5	all my problems.
6	Now we have to exchange information before the
7	police arrive. May I see your license? License. *Driver's*
8	license. Little small thing tells your height and weight.
9	You use it to cash checks at the supermarket. *(Listens,*
10	*repeats.)* You're five-foot-ten, weigh 175 pounds, you like
11	fishing, poetry and folk dancing with blonde women.
12	Look, I'm not a computer dating service.
13	You want to see my license? Would you reach into
14	my back pocket? I'm sort of pinned down here. *(Goes*
15	*through motions.)* No, I'm here in the back seat. Yes, I left
16	rather suddenly.
17	Oh, glad you like the car. The upholstery was
18	prettier before those bloodstains. What do you drive? A
19	Monster Devil 16. Hmmm? Six-hundred eighty
20	horsepower. It sleeps six. Eight if you're with close
21	friends. Car that size must cost a lot to run. *(Listens,*
22	*repeats.)* In the city you get twelve miles to a tankful.
23	Right, that's my license. I'm five-foot-nine . . . I
24	know I don't look it all hunched up like that, but that's
25	my license. Yes, I have blue eyes. *(Pauses)* Why, thank you.
26	Look, no lectures. A headrest on the seat is nice
27	but it wouldn't have helped. I'm in fantastic pain. My
28	body is an encyclopedia of injuries. I do need help of
29	some type. OK, OK, I'll get a headrest.
30	*(Listens)* Yes, you've got a headrest. Relaxing. I
31	know. You lean your head back and doze. Doze while
32	driving? How do you wake up?
33	*(Listens)* An automatic wake-up device . . . the
34	sound of the collision when you whack into another car.
35	Ralph Nader might be interested, but I'd save the postage

1   if I were you.

2   I wonder if you would see fit to extricate me?
3 *(Listens, repeats.)* **You don't like my looks. Well, you would**
4 **have before the crash. OK, you don't like me personally.**

5   **Don't shout! You'll wake my wife. It's the first time**
6 **she's been quiet all day. That's her over there, sticking**
7 **out of the glove compartment.**

8   *(Facing in other direction.)* **I know, dear. I can't move**
9 **either. You can't move anything but your tongue and lips.**
10 **You're well on the road to recovery, my dear.**

11   *(Other direction — listens.)* **What's that? A cool**
12 **drink? Great. Ginger ale. Pour it right in my mouth.**

13   *(Opens mouth — gulps.)* **Smooth.** *(Toward wife —*
14 *listens.)* **OK.** *(Back to other driver.)* **Fellow, my wife wants**
15 **some ginger ale.** *(Back to wife.)* **Look, dear, he's got your**
16 **favorite kind of chips and cheese dip.**

17   **Look, friend, I know you have to leave. Love to**
18 **have you in, but the doors won't open.**

19   **Before you go. I wonder if you'd turn on my radio.**
20 **Station WOW . . . yes, the good music station.**

21   **Thanks, bud. Sorry I can't reach out to shake**
22 **hands. Take care crossing the street.**

23   **Look out! Watch it!** *(Winces at impact. Looks up, then*
24 *down. He edges over on chair to make room.)*

25   **Glad to see you again, friend. Nice having you**
26 **drop in like this.**

27   **Nonsense, there's always room for one more.**

28   **Here, have some ginger ale, chips and dip. Here's**
29 **to your health!**

30

31

32

33

34

35

#37

Power!

CAST: Monologist — male or female.

MONOLOGIST: Power is big in our society today. You have all kinds of power.

There's Nuclear power. Power lawn mowers. Power tools. Power weight-lifting. Consumer power. Power is everywhere.

When a student has a big test coming up he goes off by himself for some power thinking. When he's deep in doubt about passing that test, he goes off by himself for some power praying.

There are many kinds of power. We have a few types of power that aren't too well known. For instance . . . there is husband power.

Husband power is getting a divorce and asking your wife for a letter of recommendation.

But the wives have power, too. Wife power is steaming open your husband's mail while it's still in his pocket.

Wife power is staying in bed on Mother's Day . . . and staying there until Father's Day.

But the unmarrieds have their own particular power.

Bachelor power is throwing a Sweet Sixteen party — you and fifteen girls.

Bachelor Girl power is putting your measurements *(Phone number)* on your license plate.

Power operates on both sides of the law.

Police power is giving a ticket for littering to a man who just fell out of a ninth floor window.

Crime power is a mugger demanding a guaranteed annual wage.

There is power in all walks of life.

Doctor power is advising a playboy to give up cigarette girls.

Psychiatrist power is treating a patient for schizophrenia and sending him two bills.

Mortician power is placing a "Welcome" mat outside his funeral home.

And there's power for individuals.

Macho power is facing a firing squad and hiring a photographer to take *before* and *after* pictures.

Fat power is burning your Weight Watchers card and singing "We Shall Overeat."

Free enterprise power is a playboy operating a kissing booth in Death Valley.

And ...

Free enterprise power is writing hold-up notes for illiterate bank robbers.

And then there's power for the unusual.

Weirdo power is making a long-distance crank phone call — collect.

Freak power is a hermaphrodite dancing cheek-to-cheek with himself.

And then there is ...

Creative thinking power ... challenging a karate expert to a fight and shooting him with a high-powered rifle.

Ah ... and here's my favorite ... teacher power.

Teacher power is demanding higher salaries, longer vacations ... and combat pay.

And to everyone out there — more power to all of you.

#38

Really Cooking Now

CAST: Monologist — female. (Think Phyllis Diller for character identification.)

MONOLOGIST: If you folks are thinking of coming to my place later for dinner — forget it!

I can't cook — I ruin grapefruit.

I've tried. Lord knows I've tried. I went to school and took up remedial cooking.

Believe me, I *do* have people over. I cook, serve and count the survivors.

Eat at my place and I guarantee you'll learn how to spell *relief.*

Some people paint by numbers. I *cook* by numbers.

You should try my well-done *seven* topped by my *four* gravy with a side order of *thirteen*. It all adds up to stomach cramps.

I have speed bumps on the way to the back door.

You've never seen so many galloping gourmets.

Appearance is half of presenting appetizing dishes. Great. My spaghetti comes out looking like an explosion in a Brillo® factory.

Everything tastes like Chicken of the Swamp.

But some guests don't care about taste. Like my cousin Bertha. She visited me a few weeks back and ate everything in sight. Eats, eats, eats. And she never gains weight. Still weighs the same as she did in high school — 386 pounds.

For her birthday her family gave her a matching set of power knife and fork.

She goes to a well-known fast-food hamburger place, eats her fill and rushes outside to watch the numbers change.

The other day she bought a new outfit, bright blue and yellow. She was standing at the bus stop and three people came up and dropped rolls of film into her pocket.

The other day I took cousin Bertha out to dinner — I could afford it. I cashed a Savings Bond. In the restaurant big cousin Bertha bent over to tie her shoelace — and the waiter threw a table cloth over her.

When it comes to cooking, I usually take the easy way out. Of course, most of my TV dinners have to go back to the shop.

I've eaten so many TV dinners I can get three channels on my stomach.

At breakfast, when I make shredded wheat, it looks like I'm destroying a bird's nest.

Once I made a boiled tongue sandwich — the tongue cursed at me.

I do my best. I serve large gatherings. The other evening I put out a giant meal and one of the guests committed the ultimate blunder in dinner table etiquette — he belched. A man nearby said: "How dare you belch before my wife?"

Said the guest: "I didn't know it was her turn."

When it comes to Thanksgiving, count me out. I tried it once. I was stuffing the turkey for forty-five minutes, making no progress at all. I got so mad I almost killed it.

You all seem like nice folks. Tell you what. Why don't you all come over to my place for dinner — a friendly bit of advice — bring your own stomach pumps.

#39

Review of the St. Valentine's Day Massacre

CAST: Announcer — male or female; Monologist — male or female.

SETTING: A desk which the narrator can sit behind or lean against, whichever can be more effective as he reads or speaks his review.

ANNOUNCER: There is one person who brings together journalism with our country's cultural life — the critic.

Critics review drama, literature, television, opera, musical soloists, political speeches, restaurants, night clubs, cook books, ecological programs, athletic events, comedians, everything. Just about. There's one aspect of American life that has been overlooked by our critics.

It is our nation's fastest-growing indoor and outdoor sport — crime. We must accord it the attention it merits.

Oh, I don't mean your simple off-off-Broadway crimes like molesting a meter maid or contributing to the delinquency of a sleep walker.

It's the big crimes that need reviewing. It's bound to happen. We will soon read and hear critiques of our major crimes — crimes like the St. Valentine's Day Massacre. *(Spotlight switches to MONOLOGIST.)*

MONOLOGIST: Hi, crime buffs. This is your social critic Edgar *(EDWINA)* Societal with our review of the week.

What will undoubtedly become one of our most controversial crimes opened last night in a garage on Chicago's Clark Street.

It was called the "St. Valentine's Day Massacre," and this production, truly an authentic drama of social revolution, will be talked about for years to come.

Expository scenes detailing the internecine gang warfare of the city's top crime factions were brief and in no way slowed the pace of this valuable human document set against the stark background of the Doran gang's bootlegging headquarters. Setting by the SMC Cartage Company was superb.

Suspense built slowly but steadily, leading to the climactic scene when the protagonists entered, machine guns in hand, and quickly cross-ventilated their rivals before making an ambling, stop-action, almost too-casual, but highly dramatic exit.

Cast in the role of Chief Killer, was Legs Bubblekopf, long recognized as one of crimedom's up-and-coming torpedoes. This is his first major outing and he carries off his role as high executioner with realistic bravado perfectly suited to the drama.

Leg's supporting cast of killers carried on in capable, business-like fashion, especially Billy "Dum Dum" Yusker, making his debut here. At one point, a member of the chorus lined up against the wall, departed from the script and tried to escape, forcing Billy to ad-lib. The neophyte did so in professional style, pirouetting gracefully and dispatching the wayward performer with a quick, accurate volley from his Thompson sub. One minor complaint — the noise of the machine guns was overpowering for front row witnesses. A few dollars invested for silencers is suggested for future performances.

A word about the choreography done by Gower Berdoo. When the staccato coughing of the three machine guns exploded in the climactic scene, the seven victims over-acted with near hysteria. The kicking, twitching and screaming was strictly bush-league stuff. I'm willing to chalk it up to opening night jitters, but sincerely hope Berdoo will be able to exercise more restraint henceforth.

Costumes by Marietta of Cicero were authentic and in perfect detail right down to the slash in Biff Machismo's vest where his wife had knifed him early that morning.

There was one jarring note. In the curtain scene where Swanky Dusenberg — with fourteen slugs in his body — is dying in the arms of a police sergeant, he whispers, "Nobody shot me." No doubt this was meant to be a final, ironic touch.

However, it came over to much of the audience as unintentional humor and I heard several stifled guffaws at the moment which should have been highly charged, though subdued drama.

But I'm carping on a minor failing. Overall the drama strikes a responsive chord. It is highly informative, devoid of sentimentality and done in dramatic terms understandable to even the uninformed or occasional crime-goer. It will no doubt be imitated in all theaters of crime throughout the nation in years to come.

The author, though not identified in either the Playbill or police blotter, will be heard from again. He is a skilled craftsman and his handling of the mass-killing scene is consistently witty and rich in color.

Though faintly derivative in concept — the slayings show the influence of predecessors Big Jim Lee, Johnny T and Machine Gun McFern, the drama reveals the author to be honestly motivated and creatively daring. He is a killer to watch.

All in all, "The St. Valentine's Day Massacre" is a big hit.

#40

Doomsday Spiel

CAST: Announcer — male or female; Monologist — male. (Bob Newhart for character identification.)

ANNOUNCER: **Hardly a week goes by without some mystic, prophet or doomsayer predicting the end of the world. Often mild panic or downright hysteria ensues.**

Frightened people toss themselves into empty swimming pools, while others sell their personal belongings and flee to high ground.

Whatever happens, there is always a huckster around ready to make capital of the situation.

Let's look in on this gathering which followed the latest prediction of doom by Maharaja Maramama Marmaduke.

Addressing the crowd is Fred Huckster.

MONOLOGIST: *(MONOLOGIST addresses the audience, representing the gathering.)* **Since we're all here, I think we ought to get right down to business.**

(Listens) **Hmm? Golly jinkers, I don't know how the end will come. Flood, probably. That's the way I'm betting. But let's see what you others say.**

Who thinks the world will end by flood? Let's have a show of hands.

(Looks out and counts to himself.) **Seventeen. How many think we'll go out via the freezing route?** *(Looks out.)* **Only seven. How about fire? Hmmm? Oh, that's when the sun gets bigger and closer and it gets hotter and hotter until we just . . .** *(Listens)* **What's that? No, I don't think sun tan lotion will help.**

(Listens) **Yes, that's right, the whole world will go**

1 according to the prophet. Right, even New Jersey.
2 Our leading prophet predicted the world would
3 end today. The Russian prophets thought it already had
4 ended. Our Maharaja is one of the four original prophets
5 left after the war. Remember? We got two and Russia got
6 two. *(Listens)* Yes, you might call it a prophet-sharing plan.
7 Since we haven't much time left, let's talk turkey.
8 I have a lot of ascension robes I'm willing to let go at
9 cost. They're all certified Army and Navy surplus. As you
10 can see, *(Looks away.)* they're hanging on plain gas pipe
11 racks. Notice the pockets. You can keep two, maybe three
12 weeks' supply of survival biscuits in those.
13 How do the robes work? Very simple. Let's say
14 the end comes by earthquake. You simply warm up the
15 robe and *(Gestures with a pointed finger outward.)* press the
16 starter button right there ... *(Presses)* ooops ... sorry,
17 didn't know you were so ticklish, Miss Harrison. Not at
18 all. My pleasure. *(Big smile.)*
19 Where was I? Oh yes, you press the button and
20 you lift right off the ground and you hover until you're
21 ready to land ... if there's anything left to land on.
22 Also, of course, in New York you have to be very
23 careful of crumbling skyscrapers — always a danger. Ask
24 anybody.
25 Now I'm sure you'll agree togetherness is
26 important at this time. With that in mind I rented Legion
27 Hall from now until the end. You'll find swings, sandboxes
28 and hobby horses. In addition, there are some nice
29 amusements for the kiddies.
30 If you're interested see Miss Freebish, my
31 secretary. Ask her about our special family plan at low,
32 low rates.
33 *(Listens)* What's that, miss? Oh, golly gee. I don't
34 know. You can if you want to, but I wouldn't advise you
35 spend twenty-two dollars for a permanent right now.

1	*(Listens)* **What's that? Well, I have a sneaky hunch**
2	**we're going by flood. What I've done is equip a huge ark.**
3	**I have two geese, two ducks, two pigeons, two turkeys,**
4	**two chickens, two of just about everything.**
5	**However, I am looking for a . . . let me put it this**
6	**way . . . if there are two healthy young women between**
7	**the ages of nineteen and twenty-five, single and**
8	**interested in taking a mystery excursion to Never-Never**
9	**Land with Captain Jack, just leave your names and vital**
10	**statistics with Miss Freebish.**
11	**One more thing — if something goes wrong — I**
12	**mean if the world *doesn't* end, I'm holding open house on**
13	**the ark. Tickets are twelve bucks a head and bring your**
14	**own refreshments.**
15	**We'll have a small band for dancing, a great buffet**
16	**with geese, turkey, duck, pigeons, chicken and so forth.**
17	**See you aboard — maybe!**
18	
19	
20	
21	
22	
23	
24	
25	
26	
27	
28	
29	
30	
31	
32	
33	
34	
35	

#41

The Subway Ride

CAST: Announcer — male or female; Monologist — male.

ANNOUNCER: Psychiatrists say that one out of every eight people, though seemingly normal in appearance and behavior, is harboring a secret fear or neurosis that would classify them as mentally disturbed.

I'd go along with that. And they all appear to be so normal. Like that fellow over there who is just boarding the subway train going from Manhattan to Brooklyn under the East River. *(MONOLOGIST enters, sits down on chair. He is carrying a newspaper.)*

He's Ned Normal. Average face. Average clothes. Average everything. The subway doors close. Let's find out what's going on in his mind.

MONOLOGIST: *(MONOLOGIST looks around at fellow passengers. Shakes head.)* Look at these people. That guy over there. Got a face like a chimpanzee. Boy, you meet some beauties down here.

But subways are more interesting than cabs. Get an education. You see things. You come to grips with life. Cheaper, too.

Wonder where Elaine wants me to take her tonight. Probably some expensive restaurant. Well, that's out.

None of that fancy stuff. I'll take her to see the Empire State Building. Trouble with New Yorkers is they don't take time to see their own city's landmarks. I'll show her the sights of New York and we'll go to the top of the Empire State Building. She's not pushing me around. *(Makes face and puts finger in ear.)*

1	Ooops, there goes the ear popping. We must be
2	under water now. Lots of people get nervous along about
3	now, I bet. Like chimp face over there. Bet he's sweating.
4	Doesn't bother me though. Cool. Easy. He's tense already
5	and we're only seventy-five or eighty feet under water.
6	*(His face shows a little alarm at this thought.)*
7	Seventy-five or eighty feet! Boy, the Red Cross is
8	right. Everybody should learn to swim. You know you
9	might have to swim in a flooded subway some day. *(That*
10	*disturbs him and he pulls the newspaper out and starts reading.*
11	*Suddenly he looks up.)*
12	Oh, oh. We're stopped. Well, it happens all the
13	time. Probably letting some fish pass. They say fish have
14	the right of way. Or maybe a tugboat. Maybe lots of
15	tugboats. Maybe the tugboat hit the tunnel and it's
16	leaking and we're going to ... *(He starts to leap up in panic,*
17	*then catches himself.)*
18	What am I doing? The train stopped. So what?
19	Nothing to it. I'll say one thing about chimp face though.
20	He's hiding his panic pretty well. Well ...
21	yep ... yep ... the train is stopped.
22	*(Begins reading paper. Then looks up. Stops reading.)*
23	The train is stopped ... and the lights have gone out. Well,
24	nobody's getting panicky. Hate to have to control this
25	gang of oddballs. I would take on three or four but not
26	the whole bunch. *(Flexes arms, makes fists.)*
27	*(He start reading again. Then slams the paper aside.)*
28	Who wants to read? I want to get out of here. Where's the
29	driver? Where's the conductor? Come to think of it, he
30	was yawning when I got on.
31	*(He looks up and watches someone pass by.)* Oh, there's
32	the conductor. Still yawning. They only hire tired people
33	here? *(Shakes head.)*
34	Well, we'll be going soon and I'll see Elaine and
35	listen, baby, you go where I want to go. No bright lights

1	stuff. No, sirree. She can't push me around . . . But we're
2	not moving. Move, move!
3	Take it easy, Ned. Look at that five-year-old kid.
4	He's not nervous. Why should I be? Of course, he's never
5	lived the swinging life. Never kissed any girls . . . but I
6	have and I want to kiss more girls. *(Panicking)* I want to
7	kiss Elaine. Elaine, I'll take you anywhere. Atlantic City.
8	Hollywood. Anywhere. Elaine. *(Looks upward.)* Save me! I
9	want to live . . .
10	*(He buries his head in his hands. Looks up, now calm.)*
11	Take it easy. What am I doing? So if the train's not moving.
12	Look at the conductor, *he's* not moving. Sleeping on the
13	job, that's what he's doing.
14	Better go wake him up. No, wouldn't look good.
15	Wait until Chimp Face goes over. He's ready to crack.
16	Sure . . . he's trying to hide it behind a yawn. Oldest trick
17	in the books. Better be ready. If he blows. POW! *(Smacks*
18	*fist into hand.)* Have to deck him.
19	Well, nothing to do but wait. One good thing — if
20	we go down at least I'm not going down alone. Be a big
21	catastrophe. Headlines. Pictures in the papers. The
22	whole list of victims. My friends will get a kick out of
23	seeing my name in the papers.
24	Better than dying home in bed. Me and Chimp
25	Face going down together.
26	*(A look of panic comes over his face.)* **I don't want to**
27	**drown! I want to go home and die in bed!** So much neater.
28	*(Buries his head in his hands.)* **What am I doing?** This
29	is ridiculous. What can happen? The conductor won't let
30	me die — if he wakes up. He's a family man. If I die, he
31	comes with me. He wants to get home to his family. Maybe
32	he *hates* his family. And they hate him . . . sleeping all the
33	time. Maybe he wants to go this way. He's going and he's
34	taking me with him! *(Looks at "Conductor")* Madman!
35	OK, OK, hold it. Relax. So if it goes down, so what?

1	I'm not afraid for myself. But Elaine . . . She'll *miss* me.
2	She'll miss the nights on old Broadway, Atlantic City,
3	Hollywood, the Riviera and all the other places I'd take
4	her.
5	Take it easy, Ned. Relax. Sing. That's it. Sing a
6	song. *(He sings.)* "Many brave hearts are asleep in the
7	deep . . ."
8	*(Catches himself.)* Oops, wrong song. Let's see.
9	What's a nice tune?
10	*(He closes his eyes and runs his finger under his collar,*
11	*loosening it. He runs his hand across his forehead. He's sweating.*
12	*He brings his hand down from forehead and looks at it. He sees*
13	*sweat. He panics. He leaps up, shouting.)* The tunnel broke!
14	The river is flooding in! The dam broke! It's the East River
15	flood! We're all doomed! Doomed, do you hear?
16	*(Suddenly his head snaps back and he slams back onto*
17	*his seat. He sits there, unmoving. Then he comes to and shakes*
18	*his head.)* Hey, where am I? What happened?
19	*(He looks off and eyes widen.)* Oh, Chimp
20	Fa . . . er . . . *(Listens)* what? I panicked and you had to
21	flatten me. *(Rubs jaw.)* No . . . of course not. No hard
22	feelings. Nope. I understand. I've been working hard.
23	Under a strain. Big financial dealings. I'm talking big
24	bucks. Stress. Right. You understand.
25	*(Rubs jaw.)* Hey, the train's moving again. *(Big smile*
26	*crosses his face. He looks out the window.)*
27	We're past the river. Here's the station. Wasn't so
28	bad. Ah, we're stopping. Now where's Elaine. *(Searches*
29	*out window.)* Sure, late again. *(Irritated)* Where is that
30	chick?
31	*(He spots "Elaine." He gets up and moves off to one side.*
32	*He talk to her.)* Sure, late again. Why is it you're always
33	late? *(Listens)* OK, OK. It's OK about being late. But
34	another thing. None of this bright lights and fancy
35	nightclub bit. We're going to the Empire State Building

1 and then maybe the museum. Get some culture going.
2 *(Listens)* **What? Take the subway back to the city? You**
3 **kidding? What am I, a cheapskate or something? Not old**
4 **Ned! Let's grab a cab.**
5 **When you go with old Ned Normal, baby, you go**
6 **first-class.** *(He extends arm, "Elaine" takes it, and he walks off*
7 *smiling, confident as he exits.)*
8
9
10
11
12
13
14
15
16
17
18
19
20
21
22
23
24
25
26
27
28
29
30
31
32
33
34
35

#42

Professor Paul Pushner's Positive Approach
Personality Improvement Program

CAST: Announcer — male or female; Monologist — male.

ANNOUNCER: You've probably noticed that our land abounds in counselors. People are paid to give advice to us. And we listen. And we pay.

There are organizations to improve our personalities, give financial advice, stop stuttering, advise on legal matters and beautify us. But there's no group quite like this one — Professor Paul Pushner's Positive Approach Personality Improvement Program.

MONOLOGIST: *(He bounds on stage, very aggressive, exuberant.)* All right, listen up out there. For all you first-timers out there, I'm Professor Paul Pushner and I'm King of the Hill around here and you can be too, if you smarten up, pay attention and somehow muddle through Professor Paul Pushner's Positive Approach Personality Improvement Program. Known familiarly as the PPPPAPIP — it's pronounced just the way it reads.

(Looks out over audience.) I want to say this is a pretty nice turn out of wilted wallflowers and drooping daisies — but pay attention and I'll make you all winners — like me.

First of all, turn around and face me. Come on, it's easy. The first step all of you emotionally impoverished introverts got to take is to believe in yourself, assert yourself so you, too, can be successful.

Look at me. Do you realize I used to be a ninety-seven pound bashful kid myself. I was as backward as any of you hangdogs out there. But I learned the magic

1   secret and I'm going to tell you.

2   Now, what is the Pushner Positive Approach that
3   you skulkers are shelling out good dough for?

4   As I explained last week in my talk at the national
5   convention of hermits, I'm using a basic psychological
6   gambit — I stress greed. Greed and hatred of others.

7   Now there are three simple rules you must learn
8   if you want to get the most mileage out of your hatred.

9   Rule 1 — Know thyself. *(Stares at audience.)* For
10   some of you this is going to be a shattering experience,
11   because I know emptiness when I see it.

12   Rule 2 — Hate others.

13   Rule 3 — Hate others more.

14   If you do your homework and apply yourself you'll
15   end up hating me. If you don't, I'll know you're goofing
16   off and you'll answer to me.

17   Actually, a side benefit of this personality
18   improvement course is the fine friendships that spring
19   up. One young man ended up hating a shapely young
20   miss so much he married her. And I'm happy to say that
21   that's a happy marriage because the combatants don't
22   even speak to each other.

23   OK now, question time. Yes, miss? I can't
24   understand you. Don't cover your face. At least not with
25   your skirt.

26   What's your problem? You're so shy ... *(Leans
27   forward, straining.)* speak up ... you're so shy you blush at
28   stock car races and bingo games? Well, listen, sister,
29   before I help you out, have you paid your entire fee? No?
30   Then don't bug me. We don't work the charity bit around
31   here.

32   Feel that tingle of hate? Good. That's the first step
33   to success. Hate makes the world go round and don't
34   forget it.

35   Hate works miracles. Hate works wonders and

cures phobias. You are what you hate.

Let me tell you that aggressiveness is the key. Push yourself forward. Interrupt everybody. Speak out of turn and let them know that you're out there.

You there. The ugly kid with the unsightly blemishes. Lend me ten bucks. Right now. Good. Hey, elderly person in the corner. Hobble up here with twenty. Come on, shake it up. *(Reaches out as if accepting money.)* You there. I want fifty from you. Sense that hatred? You got to move like me.

I borrow and you don't get your money back until you're strong enough to demand I return it.

What's that, son? You want your money back? You lent me ten dollars a minute ago? Stop living in the past. See how I handled that. You can learn to do that too, and get rich overnight.

Yes, pal. What? You and your friend want the money. Who's your friend? *(Looks at waist level.)* A thirty-eight caliber revolver. *(Hands over money.)* Take the dough. Watch? Sure. *(Takes off watch.)* Jacket? *(Takes off jacket.)* Right.

Why are you all laughing? Where are you going? Come back . . . come back.

(Dials phone, talks into it.) Acme Employment Agency. Jim, just turned loose another batch of the nastiest, surliest, arrogant no-goods around. You'll be doing great business with them. They'll become some of the best, nastiest, surliest, arrogant waiters and waitresses you've ever seen. *(Smiles, hangs up phone.)*

#43

Uncle Harry Takes Nephew Ethelbert to the Zoo

CAST: Announcer — male or female; Monologist — male. (Think Jonathan Winters for character identification. He is slightly manic and there is a sense of repressed mischievous behavior, but underneath it all, a nice guy.)

ANNOUNCER: Bachelor uncles are usually envied by the rest of their family. They are considered pleasant, gregarious, care-free and good guys because they don't really have any serious family obligations. But what if that happy-go-lucky uncle is placed in an uncomfortable, unusual, unfamiliar situation — such as when good old Uncle Harry takes his little rambunctious nephew Ethelbert to the zoo.

MONOLOGIST: *(MONOLOGIST requires good facial expressions showing inner feelings and reactions to surroundings and happenings.)* **Glad we could get out to the zoo together, Ethelbert.** *(Shakes head, winces, talks aside.)* **Ethelbert. I even hate to say that name.**

If you got any questions about these animals, just ask me.

See that over there? That's a giant Galapagos turtle. Sleepy. Slow-moving. *(Listens to Ethelbert.)* **What's that?** *(Stares again.)* **You're right. It *is* a rock.** *(Chuckles)* **Just testing you.** *(He wasn't.)*

Now that's a crane, that long-legged bird. Hmmm? *(Listens)* **Why does he always stand on one leg? Really don't know. You do. Tell me.** *(Listens, repeats.)* **Because if he lifted the other one he'd fall down. OK.**

And put that pea shooter away. You almost hit that pigeon. Hey, want to feed the pigeons? Go ahead.

No, no, no! You don't feed the pigeons to the tigers! *(Shakes head.)*

And don't shoot that thing at the tigers. If they get free, they'd tear you apart. *(Looks at the annoying kid.)* Well, maybe just one shot . . . no . . . forget I said that. Put it away.

Now look at that. There's a strange one. Look at that hairy face, those long arms and those huge feet . . . oops, sorry, sir. What? Oh . . . *sorry*, madam.

Hey, how about a taffy apple? *(Goes through motions of paying out change, taking taffy apple and handing it to boy.)* Let's rest. *(He sits on chair. Looks at "ETHELBERT".)* Why are you crying? *(Listens, repeats.)* I'm sitting on your taffy apple. *(Gets up, dusts off seat of pants.)* Why are you laughing? *(Listens, repeats.)* It looks like a Cadillac tail light. *(Takes it off and throws it into basket.)*

I like the big cats. Tigers. They're the meanest cats in Africa. *(Stops, listens, repeats.)* There are no tigers in Africa? I didn't know that. *(Repeats)* The tigers are from Detroit. Clever, Ethelbert, clever. *(Aside)* I really *hate* that name.

And put down that pea shooter. Too many people around.

(He straightens up, reacts to a slap in the face.) Lady, I didn't lay a hand on you! *(Points to "ETHELBERT".)* He did it. *(Protesting)* I didn't touch you. *(She walks away.)* Give me that. *(He snatches the pea shooter away. He turns to look in the direction that the lady walked away. He smiles, nods appreciatively.)* Not bad. *(He puts pea shooter to mouth, then pulls it down fast.)* No . . . what am I doing?

This kid's driving me nuts.

Ah, look. They're going to feed the seals. *(Reaches down as if to grab the nephew by the collar and seat of the pants.)* Can you swim? *(Catches himself.)* He's gonna get me crazy.

Ah, here are some animals. Look you can ride

them. How about that. Ponies, goats. Hey, how about a nice ride on a leopard? OK, OK.

Sure, I can buy you one of those big balloons. *(Pays man, hands balloon to nephew.)* Careful, Ethelbert. They're filled with helium. They're strong. Hold tight, Ethelbert. Hate that name.

(Suddenly head jerks up. He looks up in the air with alarm.) Ethelbert. Stop fooling around. Come down! *(Panics. Reaches for pea shooter and blows shot upward. He then circles around like an outfielder and after a few seconds catches "ETHELBERT" in his arms. He sighs with relief. He puts "ETHELBERT" down and holds his hand as they start off slowly.)*

You may be a rotten, bad news nephew, but you're *my* rotten, bad news nephew, Ethelbert.

(He smiles down warmly at the nephew as they move away. Then he gets a wild-eyed mischievous grin on his face.) Hey, let's go to the amusement park. We'll cut the seat belts on all the bumper cars. Like that? I knew you would. Let's go, Ethelbert. *(Holds nephew's hand and exits.)*

#44

Down Memory Lane

CAST: Monologist — male. (If MONOLOGIST chooses, he can wear some make-up or outfit to make him appear as a middle-aged man.

MONOLOGIST: Lately, whenever I'm alone, I find myself thinking about my childhood. I guess we all do.

I had a great childhood. Lots of memories. My mother was funny.

I used to climb the back fence and walk on it like a tight-rope walker. *(Demonstrates)* Drove my mother crazy. She'd yell out the window: *(Shouts)* "Hey, whatsa da matter, you a crazy?"

"Why do you talk like that, mom? You aren't Italian."

She always did have trouble with the language.

My younger brother always used to imitate me, just to annoy me. And it did. I got sore. I told my mother, "Ma, Jimmy's always imitating me, doing everything I do."

She told him: "Jimmy, stop acting like a fool!"

And you all can look back and remember the bashful guy in the crowd. There's always one. My bashful friend was Herkimer. He used to comb his hair, press his pants and get a manicure — just to call a girl on the phone.

He was shy because he really didn't know what to talk about with a girl. Just kept silent. When he walked with a date he'd toss rocks around. *(Gestures tossing rocks.)*

The prettier the girl, the harder he threw the rocks. *(Winds up and heaves a rock.)* One time he was going

1	with this girl named Diane. Lovely girl. I mean when he
2	was with Diane it wasn't safe to sit on the front porch.
3	He and Diane lasted a while. It was a seven-window
4	romance.
5	One day he made a mistake. He walked Diane past
6	a greenhouse. Those rocks started flying a mile-a-minute.
7	You can guess what he did to that greenhouse. Well,
8	Herkimer was arrested for vandalism. Broke his spirit.
9	He never married. But he's doing OK, though. Today he
10	is president of the National Association of Hermits. He
11	called a convention last month — and nobody showed up.
12	I went out with a couple of girls. I remember them
13	all. Mostly Nancy. Yeah. Big tall Nancy. So tall she sat
14	down in sections.
15	Not the prettiest girl. Had buck-teeth. When she
16	bit into a sandwich she gave it deckle edges. Wore braces.
17	So did I. One evening we were sitting on a park bench.
18	We kissed. It was my first kiss. An electrical storm came
19	up suddenly. Our braces locked. Lightning flashed. My
20	first kiss was really shocking.
21	She had lovely hair — for a while. One day she
22	put her hair up in a bun, fell asleep and her pet cocker
23	spaniel nibbled her bald-headed. Bald or not, she was my
24	favorite.
25	And then there was Shirley. Very fashion-
26	conscious. Wore monogrammed Supphose™ — all the
27	way up to her neck. *(Demonstrates)*
28	Shirley was the first girl in the neighborhood to
29	buy those stockings with a clock in them. But nobody
30	ever asked her for the time. It was a shame. She became
31	sad, lonely, frustrated.
32	All on account of that clock in her stocking. She
33	was tense, got all wound up and busted a mainspring.
34	She spent three years recuperating in a wild clock
35	sanctuary.

But I heard she turned out OK. She married a sun dial mechanic and now works part-time as a stage manager for a successful team of dancing dentists.

And there was always the Rich Kid. Ours was Edgemont. Edgemont the Wealthy.

He was spoiled. You know how kids write things on fences? Well, his mother bought him rubber stamps with all the words and poems printed on them. So Edgemont didn't have to go through all the trouble of writing on walls — he just stamped *(Gestures stamping.)* them on. Things like:

Roses are red, violets are blue
I'm a schizophrenic, so am I

I remember once I went to Edgemont's home. The butler had a butler. The house was immense. The living room was separated from the dining room by a river. The bathroom had a drawbridge, which led to some strange situations, as you can imagine.

I felt fortunate to know him. To be his friend you had to pass a Civil Service exam.

From what I hear, he's still interested in the power of words. He had a whole new set of rubber stamps made — big ones — and he does bumper stickers for hearses. Right. Only for hearses.

I saw some of them: "Honk twice if you liked me." "This is my first time." "Don't go away, I'll be right back."

Well, they say you can't go back again, but I'm going to try.

(Looks at watch.) Going to meet my favorite from long ago — Nancy. Ah, here she is.

(He looks up at where face of tall girl might be.) **Nancy. Your hair grew back. Like it? Love it. Green is in this year.** *(Listens, repeats.)* **Yes, a lot like neon. Green neon. Like a drugstore sign.**

(Starts off looking up.) **Let's go someplace and talk**

1	**over old times. Maybe we can create some new memories.**
2	*(He walks off, smiling happily.)*
3	
4	
5	
6	
7	
8	
9	
10	
11	
12	
13	
14	
15	
16	
17	
18	
19	
20	
21	
22	
23	
24	
25	
26	
27	
28	
29	
30	
31	
32	
33	
34	
35	

#45

Reading Your Local Newspaper

CAST: Monologist — male or female. (MONOLOGIST can carry out a newspaper as a script delivery aid. He can turn the paper over as he switches categories he announces as the bit progresses, whatever is comfortable.)

MONOLOGIST: I get a kick out of reading my local newspaper. Not the headlines, now. They can be ghastly. I mean the small bits and pieces of human interest, the advice columns, the classified ads and the fillers, those little nuggets of information used to fill up the paper's column. Things like this:

(Reads) Do you know that if the half-dollar coins minted in the United States since 1934 were stacked atop one another it would make a very tall pile?

Confucius is considered one of the greatest philosophers of all time even though he couldn't speak a single word of English.

The finest mohair comes from Kansas City, MO.

There is more nutrition in one chocolate bar than in an entire set of airline luggage.

And those little news briefs about people, places and things. They don't make the headlines but they inform you about what's going on in the world.

(Reads) St. Louis — The National Civil Liberties Union has won the right for a government employee to wear a beard on the job. Shirley Barnes is very pleased with the decision.

(Reads) Emporia, Kansas — The Roundabout Social and Garden Club held its weekly meeting

1	Thursday as usual despite a tornado which ripped
2	through the town killing nine people, none of whom were
3	club members.
4	Chicago — The housing situation is so desperate
5	here that in order to provide more living space, Mayor
6	Grinswold is renting out the vacant stare in his eye.
7	New York — Rapidly becoming known as Smog
8	City East, New York has established a daily bulletin
9	concerning the air quality. The reports tell listeners that
10	the air is "Good," "Bad" or "Nearer My God to Thee."
11	Baltimore — The National Short People reports
12	success in their drive to get more employment for its
13	members. Last week six midgets were hired to ride
14	shotgun on supermarket shopping carts.
15	Los Angeles — Good news for old-time movie fans.
16	Remember Slim Jim MacWhim, the character actor of
17	years back? No one knew where he went after he left the
18	films. Well, he turned up today. Tall, skinny Jim
19	MacWhim today makes a nice living as a bookmark in
20	the city library.
21	Boston — Veteran thief Ed Blasedoo tried to
22	break into one house too many. Last night Blasedoo
23	entered a mansion in one of the city's fanciest suburbs.
24	As he attempted to cart away a priceless old
25	grandfather's clock, the clock struck twelve and Ed
26	Blasedoo was midnighted to death.
27	San Francisco — The National - American Hospi-
28	talization Association has put into effect a new
29	policy which covers mental breakdowns suffered by
30	people trying to understand the *old* policy.
31	And those advice columns. There's advice on
32	romance, manners, etiquette, cooking, personal health
33	like this one by Dr. Abner Zirkle.
34	*(Reads)* It's easy to relieve the stresses and strains
35	which greatly affect the daily lives of millions of

Americans. To ease those tensions and get your mind off your problems, try these suggestions:

1. Sit down at a crowded bus station and giggle at everything you hear.

2. Grab a tall, willowy girl by the ankles and snap her.

3. Hang around ugly people — you'll feel prettier.

4. Wedge your tongue into the slot of a used razor blade receptacle and enter a demolition derby.

(To audience.) Hey, he said it, I didn't.

My favorite part of the paper is the classified ads.

(Reads) For sale — love seat with training wheels. Perfect for the growing teenager.

For sale — tombstone. Very reasonable. Great bargain for a family named Duffy.

For sale — I've lost fifty pounds and would like to sell ten pairs of satin hot pants with directional signals.

For sale — Slightly used chain saw. Call 555-2345 and ask for Lefty.

And this is my favorite in the personal column.

(Reads) Lonely farmer wants to marry. Seeks wife with tractor. Must be easy to start and have wide seat.

(Folds paper, looks at audience.) Now there's a man who knows what he wants out of life . . . *(Puzzled look)* I think.

#46

Rent-A-Car

CAST: Monologist — male.

MONOLOGIST: I don't know how many of you folks do a lot of driving, but I do. I'm a traveling salesman.

I'm on the road a lot and to visit my clients, I often have to rent a car. And I can tell you there are a lot of strange rental places in our larger cities.

Take New York. *(Any large nearby city can be used.)* There's the Greenwich Village Sports Car Palace. It's the only place you can rent a beaded Jaguar with gold lamé bumpers. I went there once — briefly.

And there's the Tiny Toddlers Car Rental. Only small cars. I'm talking tiny. I walked in and a guy with a tape measure around his neck came over to measure my inseam to see if I would fit into the coupe.

And then there's the Kamikaze Kar Kompany. Oriental outfit. On the West Side. Maybe you've seen the sign outside their place — "Forget Pearl Harbor."

The showroom is packed with Edsels, Hupomobiles, Terraplanes, Rocknes, Reos, cars like that. But the Japanese have remodeled them. They put the steering wheel in the middle, so you'll be able to choose which door you want to leap from when the car goes out of control.

The rates are cheap and I was tempted, but I chickened out when they fed me a full dinner of my choice and began shaving my legs. Sort of drained my confidence right there.

Then there's the Stripped Down Clean Car Company. They don't rent style and luxury. No optionals.

Nothing fancy. For instance, most rental cars have stereos. This one has a jockey strapped under the hood who sings opera whenever you push in the cigarette lighter.

I backed out of this one, too, when I found out they had a sleep-in mechanic in the trunk.

The agencies are great, but I do have a gripe against the rates. I mean they're confusing. *(Takes out card to read from.)* Listen. This is for a Plymouth Heroic Homer Hugger.

(Reads) Hourly three-hour minimum, four dollars. Business day Monday to Friday, eight a.m. to six p.m., $11.90. Overnight special Sunday to Thursday, five p.m. to nine a.m., $13.00. Twenty-four hour Weekday and Sunday, five p.m. to Friday Noon, $19.00. Twenty-four hour Friday Noon to Sunday, five p.m., holidays (like Ralph Nader's birthday), $28.15. Weekend Friday Noon to Monday, nine a.m., $72.00. Business week, Sunday, five p.m., Friday, five p.m., $62.55, weekly — any seven consecutive days, (with two days off for good behavior) $130.

Now that's for the Heroic. For the Dodge Javelin Jumping Jack, which is about the same type of car, you add fifty cents on the hourly, a dollar on the business day and the overnight special, twenty-four hour weekday and three dollars for the weekend, business week and weekly rates. Go to Jail, Go Directly to Jail, Do Not Pass Go.

(Speaking to audience.) Well, it really is like a game.

(Back to reading.) If you want a Chevrolet Ack-Ack Backpack model, it's fifty cents more than the Dodge, but fifty cents less than the full-size convertible — (full-size means it hasn't been smashed yet) and one dollar less than a station wagon with three kids and a dog left in from the last driver.

1	Naturally, there's insurance. *(Can speak directly or*
2	*read.)* **Full coverage collision protection is available to**
3	**all at three dollars per day for cars and four dollars for**
4	**trucks. This is understandable, because in case you crash**
5	**into a house, the truck will go completely through, while**
6	**your standard sedan will stop at the bathroom every time.**
7	**That's a known engineering fact.**
8	**All in all, renting a car is a pretty good deal. So**
9	**if you're planning on renting one remember . . .**
10	*(Reads from card very quickly.)* **Plymouth Heroic**
11	**business week, $62.55, Dodge Javelin, three dollars more**
12	**for the business week or $65.55; Chevrolet Ack-Ack**
13	**$66.05; Pontiac Push Pull, $80.40; business week,**
14	**convertible, $81.05, any front-wheel drive truck, seventy**
15	**dollars a week, fifteen dollars a day, forty-eight dollars**
16	**Friday to Sunday, except February, which has twenty-**
17	**eight.** *(Shakes head, rubs eyes.)* **Sorry. Got carried away.**
18	**But there you have the rates. Hope it helps.**
19	*(Squints at card.)* **Hold it. There's something else.** *(Reads).*
20	**All rates quoted are subject to change without**
21	**notice.**
22	
23	
24	
25	
26	
27	
28	
29	
30	
31	
32	
33	
34	
35	

#47

The Finest Restaurants Around

4
5

CAST: Monologist — female. (MONOLOGIST can be sort of a snooty type, rather disdainful at times, but mostly a sense of self-appreciating chic.)

SETTING: MONOLOGIST is seated at a table with reports of her restaurant reviews which she can read. A phone is on the table next to her.

MONOLOGIST: Hi, this is your woman in the restaurants, Gail Gustatory, with a look at the nicer restaurants in our area.

A lot of residents of the area and visitors are not aware of the quality restaurants which abound here. Now I don't mean places like the sleazy sea-food restaurant which shall go nameless because it is being sued. One of it lobsters mauled three diners, causing severe injuries.

Or the so-called Symphony Music Box Dining Hall. Music? Bad. Last week a waiter dropped a tray of silverware and three couples got up to dance.

Not those joints, dear listeners. I'm talking style. Here's a run-down of the upper-level eateries in our area.

Let's start with *Johnny the Referee's Restaurant.* If you like action with your food, this is the place. All the waiters are punchy ex-fighters and you should see the wild fun when Johnny rings the dinner gong. It's a riot. If you over-eat and collapse on the floor, you must take a mandatory eight-count. There is a one-minute wait between courses.

Specialty of the house is pound cake. It's pounded to your order by seven ex-middleweight contenders.

1	Other recommended items are canvasback duck and
2	satin elephant trunks.
3	*Weirdo's Harbor* — Situated at the corner of
4	Havermeyer and Frenzy streets, this colorful bistro
5	features well-known whack-outs who are given to
6	frenzied fits at mid-meal and are tossed out regularly in
7	those neat-fitting, well-tailored white jackets with no
8	sleeves. Every Monday a guest weirdo starts the
9	festivities by throwing out the first quiet, well-behaved
10	diner. Try their two-decker Schizo Sandwich. If you get
11	there on a Wednesday you'll enjoy the entertainment
12	when two trustees from the state farm play badminton
13	using a live parakeet.
14	*Benny's Place* — Another spot with a simple name
15	that attracts celebrities. El Brendel, Henry Armetta,
16	Sliding Billy Watson and Johnny Downs have all eaten
17	here — once. It's known for its geographical specialties
18	which include the Rock-Ribbed Coast of Chow Mein and
19	Roast Long Island Tear Duct. For a rare treat, try the
20	double breast of raincoat. No floor show, but every twenty
21	minutes a buxom waitress in a snug-fitting uniform
22	strolls slowly through the room.
23	*Patch Morgan's Treasure Chest* — For rare
24	excitement, see patch Morgan's Treasure Chest. Patch,
25	or Madeline, as she is known to her customers, is a
26	charming hostess. The much-married Madeline — she
27	has had seven first mates, three brigands and two cabin
28	boys among her ex-husbands — is a charming wit. A
29	patron asked, "What's a buccaneer?" Retorted Madeline:
30	"A buccaneer is a very high price to pay for corn." In a
31	striking high seas decor, food is served by real pirates
32	on flaming swords. Try their breaded veal *cutlass* or
33	skinned knuckles of waterfront brawler. In keeping with
34	the decor, patrons eat their meals with genuine pirate
35	hooks supplied by Patch herself.

We know you'll enjoy *Ma Lizenbee's Hash House.* If you like simple fare, we recommend this place, which serves old American food. When Ma gets rid of it, she'll start serving *new* American food. Ma, an ex-English teacher, serves a dessert specialty — *synonym* buns, with a vintage split of infinitive, for you to swiftly drink.

Last but certainly not least, is the *Clandestine Room* of the *Hotel Hideaway.* Seeking an intimate spot where you can express yourself in endearing terms? This is it. Soft lights, soft music and softer waitresses add to the romantic mood. Speciality of the house is curved leg of showgirl. Kosher cuisine in candlelight setting. Your chance to enjoy a knish in the dark.

And that's it for our restaurant roundup tonight, food fans.

(She picks up phone, dials and speaks into it.) **Harry?** Gail. Make me up a double order of Vienna sausage, Danish ham, Swedish meatballs, Greek olives, Italian hot sauce and some French custard for dessert. Right. *(Hangs up phone.)*

Ah, now I can enjoy some real American food.

1

2

3 # #48

4

5 ## Pet Peeves

6

7 *CAST:*   Monologist — male, preferably, but female OK.

8 MONOLOGIST: I don't think I'm any different than anybody
9 else out there. Things upset me. We all have our own pet
10 peeves. I know I have mine.
11 When I'm out driving and need directions I ask a
12 man at the corner, "How do I get to Route 101?"
13 He looks at me: "From here?"
14 No, I was going to take the scenic route along the
15 Mississippi River and then shoot back to 101.
16 How do you figure?
17 And in the supermarket. You pick up a box of
18 cookies and look for place where the price is printed.
19 You turn one side of the box up. It says: "Open other
20 end." Right? You turn it around to the other side. What
21 does it say? Right. "Open other end." That gets me.
22 And how about those helicopter traffic reports
23 you get when you're driving along on the parkway,
24 trapped in tons of metal and fumes and noxious exhaust
25 and you're creeping along at seven miles an hour.
26 You turn on the radio to hear the traffic report.
27 *(Becomes helicopter pilot.)* **"Traffic on the Seaside**
28 **Parkway is moving right along at a good rate. I'd say**
29 **moderate to heavy traffic."**
30 *(Back to himself.)* **Moderate to heavy?** *(Points up.)*
31 Up there it's moderate to heavy! Down here you sit and
32 sweat for hours. Who they kidding? I mean that bugs me.
33 And while you're trapped in metal in ninety-
34 degree heat they come on with a Stay-Fresh deodorant
35 commercial! That'd bug anybody.

But my big beef are these television "newsbreakers."

Hey, you're home, watching a ballgame or a good comedy show and some fancy hair-do pops onto the screen. Why? He's got an "urgent" news announcement.

It's another *potential* outbreak of trouble in South America. I'm interested, sure, but later. Tell me later. But no, they want me to know *right now*. You guys have your own news show in its own time. Tell me then. Let me enjoy my programs.

And so much brutal stuff graphically described. A sixty-five-year-old auto mechanic is brutalized in mid-town. This comes on usually at lunchtime. Imagine what that does to your stomach? Come on, gang, back off. Let me sip my soup and munch my lunch in peace.

Did I choose to hear that story right now? No! A newsperson chose the time to upset me. Ah, there's one of their words to toy with. Newsperson. Does that bug you? When an explosion occurs in a Manhattan street, what goes flying through the air? Manholes? No. *Personholes*. Beautiful.

An eighty-year-old aunt of mine was watching a soap the other day and this smiling fellow interrupted to report a "bad earthquake" in South America. Ruined my aunt's show. Loused up an eighty-year-old lady's private afternoon leisure. And are there any "good" earthquakes?

The interruptions of free time bug everybody.

And another guy who gets me is the intruder who fancies himself a "political analyst." "Political analyst" — that's journalese for "your guess is as good as mine, but I'm in Washington, so there."

My ballgame was interrupted by a fervent, heated staccato voice intoning: "The clean air bill in Congress seems sure to pass. Of course," he added, "this is pure speculation."

You like that? Don't interrupt with speculation. Back off. Let me lead my own private life. I mean their whole pushy attitude gets me. Do they listen? No. You guys have cheapened the term "hard news."

They go on and on under various names. News previews. Special report. News flash. Bulletin. Newsbreakers. Hey, I'll get *all* the news later. At my own time. The whole story is available to me ... it's in something called a newspaper.

I pick and choose the time and news I want to read. Hey, that's freedom. Right? The American way.

Hey, fellows, getting your air-time exposure is great when salary negotiation time rolls around, but don't get rich at *my* expense.

What do you say, gang?

Give us a "no news" break.

You'll feel better for it — I know I will.

#49

Stories Granny Likes to Tell

CAST: Announcer — male or female; Monologist — female. (Jonathan Winters' character Maude Frickert might be used as character identification. The MONOLOGIST can dress up in an outfit which would help her immediate recognition. She also can pull out all stops as she cracks her way-out and far-fetched play on words.)

ANNOUNCER: We all know of grandmothers who weave tales of long ago. Stories with humor, stories with great interest and mostly, stories with a moral. There are many grandmothers who tell wonderful stories of the past, but there is no storyteller quite like our own Granny Goodness.

MONOLOGIST: *(Seated on chair as if talking to a group of children gathered about her.)* **All right, listen up, youngsters, if you want to hear another story. Today's tale is about music. As a hobby among young folk, music is rated eight on a scale of one to ten.** *(Cackles a bit.)* **A little humor there.** *(Repeats)* **Scale ... music. Just wanted to start things off on the right note.** *(Hand over mouth apologetically.)* **Oops, there's another one.**

    Moving right along. This story is about a famous composer and fiddler from Russia named Boris Vellanoff, who wrote the famous song "Oh Give Me a Home Where the Mos-cow Boys Roam."

    Vellanoff played a violin. His wife Mischka also played the violin for a while, but she gave it up — for *Stradivarius* **reasons.**

    You all know that a violin is a small stringed instrument which is tucked under the chin, much in the

manner of a napkin. Of course, it's difficult to play a tune on a napkin. On the other hand, try to wipe your mouth with a violin. That won't win you many new friends in a restaurant.

Vellanoff — you remember him — was the hit of Europe. He played the Waltz of the Vaults on Paris' Left Bank; in Milan, Italy, he favored his audiences with his own *Pizza*catto with Anchovies and in Holland he composed "When Your Tu-lips Are Close To Mine."

I quote that "Vellanoff makes his violin sing like a bird." That was from a critic in the Canary Islands. But he wasn't going out on a limb — Villanoff was truly a smash on his European tour.

However, as it sometimes does, vanity sets in and Vellanoff, instead of his usual humble self, became arrogant, conceited and disdainful to all those about him. His audiences frowned with disfavor on his antics which got so bad that in Hungary he made a *Buda*-pest of himself.

Still, he was famous all over Europe. But Vellanoff wasn't satisfied. He wanted world-wide fame. The only thing to do was to book an American tour. Yes, that was it. Tour America. The land of opportunity.

Concerts. Television. Public appearances. He would throw out the first resin bag when baseball season opened. He would endorse non-violent toys for gifted children — "Bows Without Arrows." He would write a weight control book called "Fiddle Your Fat Away."

Fame and money would all be his. He could do whatever he wanted. Vellanoff would tour America with his violin — no strings attached.

Vellanoff toured the leading concert halls, night clubs, parking lots and bowling alleys in famous cities like Secaucus, New Jersey, Akron, Ohio and Fargo, North Dakota. Then, finally, he was booked to give a concert in yes, kiddies, you guessed it — Carnegie Hall!

Thousands of tickets were sold. It would be a sell-out. Vellanoff and his entire company would make millions. His touring company became nervous at the thought of Vellanoff playing Carnegie Hall.

They began nit-picking about little things. They complained about everything the supreme virtuoso did. They complained about his clothing, his nervous habits, the way he combed his hair, his choice of sneakers, his leather cummerbund, everything. He just wanted solitude.

Finally, all this nagging and whining got to be too much for this master violinist. When opening night came, Vellanoff rose to his full height — full because he had just eaten a big meal — and announced he would not go on. He would not play the concert. The pressure they put on him was just too much. With a grand flourish, Vellanoff snapped his bow and smashed his violin over the head of a squeaky clarinet player and never played a note of music again — all because of his nagging, pestering, pushy friends. Poor Vellanoff — all he wanted was privacy.

So this is Granny Goodness bringing you the moral of the story — Always Leave Vellanoff Alone.

#50

Phobias, Anyone?

CAST: Monologist — male. (MONOLOGIST has to be calm and
sure of himself as he starts, turning into a near-manic as he
departs after describing the nature of the rare phobias.)

MONOLOGIST: A recent report stated that more than three
of ten people in this country are suffering from some
kind of abnormal fear or phobia. Frankly, I think the
number is much higher. I think most people suffer from
a phobia, whether it be a major phobia or a little-known
one.

I consider myself fortunate. I'm one of the few
people who don't have a phobia. I take things in stride.
Nothing really bothers me.

But I'm unusual. Take acrophobia — the fear of
height. How many out there are afraid of being way above
ground? *(Counts)* Right. And I know there are some out
there who have claustrophobia — afraid of being in a
tight, confining closed-in place. *(Nods)* See?

And there is autophobia — fear of being alone.
And agorophobia — fear of wide open spaces. Those are
some of the better known ones. But there are numerous
rare phobias that many people have been afflicted with,
whether they know it or not.

*(He goes through descriptive motions as he enumerates
each phobia.)* Take *Phonophobia* — fear of getting your
finger caught in a phone slot trying to retrieve your coin.
(Gestures)

And then there's *Apiphobia* — now that's the
unnatural fear of being jabbed by a bayonet in a crowded
elevator. *(Moves as if avoiding a bayonet.)*

Aichmologphobia — not many people know that

that is the abnormal fear of finding a bumble bee in your potato salad. *(Eating motion and then a look of fear and apprehension.)*

Blastaphobia — well, that's self-explanatory. Blastaphobia is the abnormal distaste of sitting down in a mine field.

Here's an unusual one. *Ophibiophobia* — abnormal fear of suddenly discovering you've used a python to keep your pants up. *(Appropriate movements.)*

And there's *Chickshoutaphobia* — that is an inordinate fear that the sky is falling. *(Calls)* "The sky is falling! The sky is falling!" You remember that one. It was in all the fairy tale books. But it's happening today. People are afraid of it. *(Gestures, looking upward, nervous twitch, bites lip.)*

Here's a new one — *Verdanohugophobia* — psychotic dread of the Jolly Green Giant — or any of the Chicago Bears.

Some of these come right home to you. *Cleansophobia* — now that's the unnatural fear of being hit in the face with a wet mop. *(Reaction to being hit.)*

And that, of course, is aggravated by *Terpsicleansophobia* — the feeling that you can't stop dancing with a wet mop because you think it's a tall, slim blond with stringy hair. *(Dancing motion and a few of the nervous tics, gestures and motions he used before as they have a cumulative effect on him, as he takes quick glances skyward.)*

Here's one that I'm sure most of you men out there have — *Glimglamaphobia* — know what that is? It's the inordinate desire to be surrounded by many beautiful women. *(Eyes widen, looks around. Nods knowingly to audience.)* **Right guys?**

And of course that's followed up very often by *Antiglimglamaphobia* — the fear that you will be *cured* of your *Glimglamaphobia*.

1　　　　　　But to all of you phobia sufferers, please let me
2　　　extend my sincerest sympathies — it must be quite a
3　　　burden to bear. *(Slight gestures.)*
4　　　　　　Oh ... one　　more ... it's　　called　　*Larynxavco-*
5　　　*caphobia* — now　　that's　　the　　fear　　of　　*(Gets　hoarse.)*
6　　　losing ... your　　ability　　to　　*(Whispering)*　　speak
7　　　properly ... that　　your　　voice　　box ... *(Gets　softer.)*　is
8　　　ruined ... and ...
9　　　　　　*(He begins shouting in manic fashion as if to compensate*
10　　*for his own voice loss, while accompanying his shouts with the*
11　　*cumulative nervous gestures from before. Shouts.)* **Hey, you,**
12　　**pull over and let me see your license! And you, the fellow**
13　　**right there with the Army boots — out of the pool! And**
14　　**all you wise guys out there, this is the intensive care**
15　　**unit — stop stepping on those hoses.** *(Starts off in a fiercely*
16　　*manic manner, gesturing and shouting all the while.)* **Hey,**
17　　**doc ... doctor! Your couch is on fire! Where do I lie down?**
18　　**Doc ... help me ... help me, Doc! The sky really *is* falling!**
19　　*(Races, twitching all the way to his exit.)*
20
21
22
23
24
25
26
27
28
29
30
31
32
33
34
35

NOTE:　The numerals running vertically down the left
margin of each page of dialog are for the convenience of
the director. With these, he/she may easily direct attention
to a specific passage.

ABOUT THE AUTHOR
Bill Majeski
(1927-1993)

"A writer's writer" is perhaps the quickest way to describe the literary vitality and versatility of the late Bill Majeski. He was a staff writer for the Johnny Carson Tonight Show, script writer for other stage comedians, and a journalist of wide experience. Over many years Bill excelled as a reporter, feature writer, and city editor of several big city newspapers. He won Newspaper Guild writing awards along with many professional accolades. Though his work days were always full of demanding deadlines, Bill managed additionally to write twenty-two published plays and four nonfiction books for major publishers.

Though his achievements in both the literary and semipro sports worlds were exceptional, Bill never lost his humility or sense of humor. When asked about his abilities as a public speaker, he said, "The other day I spoke wittily, articulately, eloquently and forcefully — unfortunately, I was alone at the time."

Order Form

Meriwether Publishing Ltd.
P.O. Box 7710
Colorado Springs, CO 80933
Telephone: (719) 594-4422
Website: www.meriwetherpublishing.com

Please send me the following books:

_____ **50 Great Monologs for Student Actors** #BK-B197   **$12.95**
by Bill Majeski
A workbook of comedy characterizations for students

_____ **Winning Monologs for Young Actors**   **$14.95**
#BK-B127
by Peg Kehret
Honest-to-life monologs for young actors

_____ **Encore! More Winning Monologs for**   **$14.95**
Young Actors #BK-B144
by Peg Kehret
More honest-to-life monologs for young actors

_____ **The Flip Side #BK-B221**   **$12.95**
by Heather H. Henderson
64 point-of-view monologs for teens

_____ **Spotlight #BK-B176**   **$12.95**
by Stephanie S. Fairbanks
Solo scenes for student actors

_____ **Get in the Act! #BK-B104**   **$14.95**
by Shirley Ullom
Monologs, dialogs, and skits for teens

_____ **Theatre Games for Young Performers** #BK-B188   **$16.95**
by Maria C. Novelly
Improvisations and exercises for developing acting skills

These and other fine Meriwether Publishing books are available at
your local bookstore or direct from the publisher. Use the handy
order form on this page.

Name: _____

Organization name: _____

Address: _____

City: _____ State: _____

Zip: _____ Phone: _____

❑ **Check Enclosed**

❑ **Visa or MasterCard #** _____

Signature: _____   *Expiration Date:* _____
       (required for Visa/MasterCard orders)

Colorado residents: Please add 3% sales tax.
Shipping: Include $2.75 for the first book and 50¢ for each additional book ordered.

❑ *Please send me a copy of your complete catalog of books and plays.*